D0112393

Practicing Exile

The Religious Odyssey
of an American Jew

Marc H. Ellis

Fortress Press
Minneapolis

PRACTICING EXILE
The Religious Odyssey of an American Jew

Copyright © 2002 Augsburg Fortress. All rights reserved. Except for brief quotations in critical articles or reviews, no part of this book may be reproduced in any manner without prior written permission from the publisher. Write: Permissions, Augsburg Fortress, Box 1209, Minneapolis, MN 55440.

Cover image: *The Last Snow,* William C. Palmer, 1956. Copyright © 2001
    Smithsonian American Art Museum. Gift of the Sara Roby Foundation.
    Used by permission.
Cover and book design by Ann Delgehausen.
Author photo by Charles Martin. Used by permission.

Library of Congress Cataloging-in-Publication Data
Ellis, Marc H.
  Practicing exile : the religious odyssey of an American Jew /
Marc H. Ellis.
     p. cm.
  ISBN 0-8006-3443-8 (alk. paper)
    1. Ellis, Marc H. 2. Spiritual biography. 3. Jews—United States—
Biography. 4. Jewish scholars—United States—Biography. 5. Palestinian
Arabs—Civil rights. 6. Judaism—20th century.
7. Spiritual life—Judaism.   I. Title.

BM755.E627 A3 2001
296'.092—dc21
[B]   2001051085

The paper used in this publication meets the minimum requirements of
American National Standard for Information Sciences—Permanence of
Paper for Printed Library Materials, ANSI Z329.48-1984.

Manufactured in the U.S.A.   AF 1-3443
06   05   04   03   02   1   2   3   4   5   6   7   8   9   10

To Aaron Moore and Isaiah Dylan,
traveling Jews in the new diaspora

—from your father, with love

Contents

Exile, the home I have with God
God, the home I have in exile

Preface

THIS MEMOIR RECOUNTS MY RELIGIOUS ODYSSEY, a search for Jewish identity and authenticity, even while "practicing exile." I am trying in these pages to understand what it means to be Jewish in the world and in our time. Although not overtly about politics or the Middle East or global economic structures, these realities figure in my search. What, after all, does it mean to be Jewish when helicopter gunships become the defining witness of Jewish life?

Two haunting images stay with me as I survey my own journey and the contemporary landscape of Jewish life. The first is Jews of conscience walking slowly into exile. For the most part, these Jews are secular, at least in their self-definition. In my mind's eye they are carrying the covenant with them.

The second image involves the Ark of the Covenant, biblical in origin and now the center of the modern synagogue. In the Ark are the Torah scrolls, covered in decorated cloth and removed from the Ark with prayers and solemnity, to be read and pondered during the synagogue service. As I look toward the Ark, my mind sees two Torah scrolls in the background and in the foreground a helicopter gunship. As a liturgical symbol, the helicopter gunship is stripped of its menacing physicality. Like the body of Christ in Christian worship, the helicopter gunship is cleaned up, silver, sleek, and gleaming.

I write these words after the first anniversary of the second Palestinian uprising that began in September 2000, and in the aftermath of the September 11, 2001, terrorist attacks on New York City and Washington, D.C. Contrary to public pronouncements and commentary, these events have not changed everything. Rather, they make more urgent the themes I address in this book. The use of helicopter gunships by the Israeli military, hovering over defenseless Palestinian cities, towns, villages, and refugee camps, and firing rockets to destroy the Palestinian governmental infrastructure and assassinate its political leaders, accelerates the decline of Jewish ethics and renders even more difficult the embrace of Jewish identity as a compelling force in the world. In the wake of September 11, Americans feel a new sense of urgency about security and safety. But few ask how we as Americans contribute to the cycle of violence. Few Jews understand that the terror we feel has been felt by Palestinians for decades.

In these pages I ponder the future of Jewish life, characterized by an exile that is unrelenting and by an increasing violence at its heart. I do not pretend an objectivity or seek to place myself above those I have encountered on this journey, even those I criticize. Walter Brueggemann, David Hartman, and the Jewish renewal movement—including Michael Lerner and Arthur Waskow—have taught me much about the foundations and expression of Jewish life. Others I have encountered on this journey, from Dorothy Day and Daniel Berrigan to Rosemary Radford Ruether and Gustavo Gutiérrez, are also open to critical analysis beyond my own. They, like myself, are flawed.

I believe that it is in the give-and-take of life and history that our fidelity is honed. In the end, as in an anthology of writing, we are part of a larger body of work, a community of many, all struggling to be faithful, all limited and flawed, but still with our individuality intact. Finding our own voice is necessary and important. It is part of our destiny.

I make no claims about the ultimate meaning of an exilic life or even the practice of exile I share in these pages. Many years ago I found myself living within two definitions of history. The first, by James Joyce: "History is a nightmare from which I am trying to awake." The second, from Martin Buber: "History is a mysterious approach to closeness." These definitions remain with me.

In my daily prayer I thank God for making me a Jew. I also thank God for calling me to be free.

What does it mean to be Jewish and to be free? I am grateful for the home I have found with God in exile. As I will recount in these pages, it is within struggle and pain that hope and fidelity emerge. It is this fidelity that I bequeath to my children.

Introduction

LIKE MANY CONTEMPORARY JEWS, I live a life of exile. An exilic life is difficult to choose and even more difficult to live. And since the Jewish exiles of our day tend to be relatively affluent and successful, it is even more awkward, perhaps even presumptuous, to claim this designation. Nonetheless it is the case, as I hope to elucidate in the following pages.

When Jews in exile begin to relate to other exiles more deserving of the appellation, the possibility of a diaspora community comes into view. As an exile who travels this diaspora, I know firsthand the difficulties that present themselves. What does it mean to be a Jew in exile? What does it mean to be Jewish in exile with other exiles from around the world? Is this another community in the making, a diaspora that contains Jews but is not Jewish? What do exile and diaspora mean for Jews and Judaism? What do the travails of exile mean for my journey and for my children?

This memoir enters the discussion of public life from an autobiographical perspective. I explore elements of a post-Holocaust journey in dialogue with the issues that confront Jews and Judaism. I also reflect on the double bind many Jewish intellectuals face. I present a challenge for Jewish inclusion in the broader tradition of faith and struggle.

There is little sense in underestimating the difficulty of responding to the challenge. This difficulty is not objective: it *is* distant and costly. Perhaps it could also be freeing. At stake is the integrity of the religious search as a truly ecumenical adventure in the twenty-first century.

Like other committed theologies across the globe, Jewish theology cannot afford an abstract stance toward identity and life. The Jewish need for engagement comes at a time when other community theologies are reflecting back on their origins and questioning their next steps. They are questioning their vision at precisely the time that we Jews are finding our tradition systematically stripped of its covenantal and ethical bases.

In my opinion, the central question of contemporary Jewish life is framed by the displacement and oppression of Palestinians. This process has been ongoing now for more than five decades. It is becoming permanent. The final sealing of the borders of an expanded Israel and the ghettoizing and fragmentation of Palestinian autonomy have arrived. There are few places in academic or public life for Jews who oppose these policies in a public way.

⌘

POST-HOLOCAUST JEWS like myself who are religious and self-critical find themselves in a dual struggle for survival. The first struggle is within the Jewish community where critical thought related to Judaism and Jewish life is frowned upon or even prohibited. The second is within the larger academic community where Jews are typically denied the expansive terrain that scholars of Christian background take for granted. The Jewish thinker and writer thus experiences a solitude because one's natural constituency and larger community both see her as suspect or out of place. A double bind is erected and the difficulty of post-Holocaust Jewish life is exacerbated.

It is less a question of privilege, ideology, or extra-scholarly identity that troubles engaged Jews like myself. Rather it is a struggle to survive the double solitude and the lack of support for a tradition that has often been demonized or romanticized but rarely engaged. Just as Christian scholarship has in many cases become a thinly veiled parallel church where innovative theology and spirituality can be explored relatively free of church authority and parishioners' needs, so, too, engaged Jewish thought needs a safe haven and a caring community where the future of Jewish life can be envisioned.

كئ

EXILES ARE FAMOUS for predicting the return to their homeland. It is
a lifelong preoccupation that betrays an underlying anxiety. If exiles
return they do so only in the physical sense. They have touched other
worlds, and the world they return to has changed as much as they
have. It is no longer their world. This is true of the architectural geography of home; it is also true of the symbolic landscape of culture
and religion. The exile loses the physical and spiritual touchstones as
known and embraced by the majority.

Most exiles will not return even in the more limited sense of land
and extended family. The gates are closed. A void lurks beyond those
gates. In the beginning of the journey the landscape is unknown and
vulnerability seems defining. Over time a landscape emerges that
seeks a new connection, this time within the context of exile. This is
the diaspora where particular backgrounds and traditions meet and
are reconfigured. There is pain in this journey. There is also hope and
possibility.

All journeys are unfinished, even when predicted and planned in
advance. So it has been—and will be—with my own life. I offer my
own journey into exile and the new diaspora as a testimony to myself
and to others. It is a memoir in the middle that builds on a chronol-
ogy yet sometimes deviates from it.

Exilic journeys defy the linear even as they seek a coherence that
is understandable to self and others. They double back and circle
around. Midlife reflections feature endings and beginnings in a variety of configurations.

In writing this memoir I re-experienced both solitude and solidarity. Aloneness permeates these reflections. But not only aloneness.
Reflection allows the gathering of life into a broader arc of vision. In
this arc I experience a peculiar sense of gratitude. Like the exile,
gratitude is difficult to explain. Originally my memoir was divided
into three parts: practicing exile, traveling the diaspora, and gratitude. The last section was the shortest.

It is difficult to offer this gratitude to others who are just beginning the journey. Can I suggest this journey to my children? Is this
the last exile in Jewish history? My sense is that it might be, but the

possibility of a Jewish future remains. The future is open. I can only struggle to be faithful in my own time. I bequeath that struggle to my children.

I am grateful for the covenant. Over time, I have become more conscious of the covenant as the foundation for my struggle and hope. Exilic journeys carry many surprises and this has been one of them. I am also grateful for those who have softened the exile through hospitality and by forgiving the flaws of personality that remain.

By speaking and writing the truth as I see it and by standing in that truth as limited and partial as it might be, I feel a strong connection with God. Once I refused belief because I was unable to define God in a satisfying way. Now I accept God without a sure definition or even the desire for one. These memoirs testify to this belief. Those who think that certainty and triumph characterize belief in God will be disappointed in my journey. So, too, will those who think that the question of God cannot be approached because of suffering and death. I am in the middle of the journey. I am also in the middle with regard to God.

In the end, however, my position is clear. When an evangelical Christian colleague defined himself a believer, I could only reply that I am as well. A friend sitting next to me suggested that the person was witnessing to me and that he would not see my belief as complete. I responded that my faith is limited, incomplete, and in need of the testimony of others—as is his. I smiled at his presumption and naïveté. I had experienced another boundary in the exile and the new diaspora.

Often I am asked about a God who judges. This question arises in the discussion of suffering, especially in relation to the perpetrators of atrocity. I doubt that a judging God exists. Still this possibility brings me to the question of a broader complicity. Jewish authorities often render judgment on Jews like myself who protest the displacement of Palestinians and the attempt to render it invisible. In conscience I cannot acquiesce in the ethical violations of the covenant that now stand at the heart of what it means to be Jewish. This issue is at *the very center of Jewish life and history*. I am ready for judgment.

The end is near. So is the possibility of new life. In these pages I try to relate how the struggle and experience of endings and new life have shaped my journey.

1

In the Beginning

IT IS TELLING that the term *worship* has meant little to me, even to the point of being off-putting. Perhaps it is the formality of the term or simply the way "worship" entered my life. It came through Hebrew school at too young an age and in a foreign language. It also came through Christian church advertisements on billboards and signs in front of imposing church structures.

Official synagogue and church ritual has always struck me the wrong way. It is as if God is boxed within a service where the seasons of religious life are known in advance and the order of prayer is the order of God. I thought this way as a child when I tried to escape the rigors of Hebrew school and Shabbat services to play sports and read. I wanted the open air and to run and play with others. To read words of history and imagination. To be free.

Hebrew school began soon after the public school day ended. Three days a week I rode my bike from school to school and then home in the dark. It was a strange and sometimes bewildering experience. In the 1950s, America's promise beckoned. My father had recently returned from World War II, and both he and my mother were busy raising a family. Growing up in a transplanted New York Jewish ethos, I was unaware of Christianity except in its commercialized appearance during the Christmas and Easter seasons. North Miami Beach seemed far away from the European Rabbinic Judaism we were learning, but we were taught this system as if it were our life's blood *and* our future.

Hebrew school was different from public school. In public school Jews were hardly ever mentioned. Only one of my teachers was Jewish and he also taught at Hebrew school. At Hebrew school we took our Jewishness for granted. Still it seemed abstracted from everyday life. We had our lives (school, sports, family), future possibilities (economic advancement, university, career)—and Hebrew school. Where did this fit into everyday life? Where would it lead us in our adult lives? Our Jewishness was emphasized and diminished at the same time. A child can make little of this dichotomy, especially when it is not recognized as a problem by his parents.

The history and language we learned deepened this dichotomy. During the day we learned about America and its future. But my identification as an American has always been a bit removed. It was almost like listening in on a history that one is joining after its formation. My relatives had come from Europe in the late 1800s and early 1900s, so we were hardly immigrants. Nonetheless, I had a sense of being an immigrant in my learning about American history. I was neither outside nor inside this history.

In the evening we learned about *my* ancestors and *my* history in the context of *our* people and history. This is the intimate history that formed us as a people and set us apart. The biblical stories and the Hebrew language are part of this journey and unique destiny. But where would this be played out in reality? The world outside of Hebrew school was a different place and an inviting one. But there was a void at the heart of that world, though it was difficult to identify it at that early age. The stories of the prophets and the haunting melodies of the Hebrew prayers accompanied me as I rode my bike home in darkness.

And then came the Holocaust. Not the event itself, for that ended before I was born, but the naming of the Holocaust as an event of significance and horror, which occurred after the end of my Hebrew school education and in my college years. In the 1950s and early 1960s, the Holocaust had not been named as yet. It was there in the background. Some of my teachers were recently arrived from Europe, but the word and the event itself were hardly spoken of. Mass death happened somewhere else; it was too horrible to speak about. Who in America wanted to hear about victims and suffering? How did you speak to children about such horror? How could I conceptualize this horror even if my teachers had a language to express it?

Once named, the Holocaust pervaded every corner of Jewish life, including my own. What did this event say to the order of worship where God is invoked with an unthinking regularity? If God has chosen us and promised to be with us, where was God in Auschwitz? And if Jesus is the savior—the redeemer of all humanity—and is present to those who are suffering, where was Jesus, himself a Jew, during each moment of loss? Where were those who followed him as their salvation?

The language of God seemed too easy to speak. And yet I was drawn to religious people, preferring their company to overtly secular people. Religious orthodoxy lacked the freedom and the questioning I needed to find my way. Secular orthodoxy struck me in a similar manner. A certainty of denial paralleled the certainty of belief.

For a long time I remained between the religious and secular, or perhaps I combined the two. Most of my life has been a search for a space and a language—a freedom—to speak of God and humanity with integrity after the Holocaust. Over the years I came to realize that I cannot find my way as a Jew or a non-Jew only, or even as a Jew or a Christian only. I need to listen to the voices of fidelity in every language, culture, and religion that I encounter. For me, fidelity, or the struggle to be faithful, is the key to spirituality. When the doors of worship are closed, the struggle to be faithful speaks to me. It is the key that unlocks the doors that often shut out religious language and ritual.

⚓

IT WAS AT THE CATHOLIC WORKER—the house of refuge and community founded by Dorothy Day and Peter Maurin in New York City in the 1930s—that I first experienced Christian worship. I had come into contact with the Worker during my college years. In lieu of graduate study, I decided to experience Worker life. The Worker is located on East 1st Street on the Lower East Side of New York City. The area is full of poor people, but I experienced people who are not just poor. Many of the Bowery people are homeless and alone, destitute rather than poor. Many have been broken by life.

As a community, the Worker volunteers live and work among the poor. They also raise their voices in critique of a social order that produces poverty. There are no programs of rehabilitation or even the offer of religious instruction as a way of regaining a foothold in life. People are free; the responsibility is within the person.

I arrived at the Worker searching for a commitment that integrated faith and social justice. In college I listened to William Miller, a professor who had written a book on the movement. I was captivated by the commitment of the people I read about and knew that my response to the Holocaust and contemporary life was uneven and inarticulate. The summer after my graduation from college I returned home and thought about flying to New York to experience Worker life. I had already made a decision to turn away from a scholarship for graduate study at an elite institution. To this day, I remember writing the letter refusing the generous offer and then standing at the mail drop, letter in hand. After mailing the letter, I turned and walked back to my apartment. I felt melancholy and uncertain. When I returned home for the summer, the uncertainty dissipated. I started to plan my journey.

I arrived on the Lower East Side of New York City in the middle of the night. The air travel was uneventful, as was the bus ride into the East Side Terminal. Then I walked the twenty or so blocks to the Worker on East 1st Street. The area was unfamiliar to me, and, coming from North Miami Beach, it looked old and uncared for. Some areas were forbidding. The sight of a twenty-one-year-old carrying two suitcases in the middle of the night to the heart of the Bowery was no doubt laughable to some of the people I passed on the street. In retrospect, my naïveté was remarkable.

I was to begin my stay across the street from the Worker in an apartment that a Worker couple occupied. When I arrived, the neighborhood was dark and relatively quiet. I heard the occasional breaking of glass from a street nearby and sirens from fire trucks several blocks in the distance. I rang the bell to the apartment and was greeted warmly. We would talk in the morning.

Worship was held in the dining room where the day meals were served to the hungry. The setting was austere and the kitchen where the meals were cooked was visible from the dining room. Religious instruction was neither demanded nor provided. The only prayers were at Mass, which was completely voluntary.

I remember sitting at the back of the room as the priest welcomed the congregation and began the Mass. The community was diverse. It included volunteers at the Worker and people who were affiliated with it in the neighborhood. Often people from the soup line attended as well. Sometimes they were communicants and other times they interrupted the Mass in need of food or clothing. Occasionally, a brick would be thrown through the window, or a person from the street, friendly when sober, would arrive drunk and angry as the words of consecration were chanted.

It was there that I met Dorothy Day, the founder of the Catholic Worker, and Daniel Berrigan, the Catholic priest who continues to present a radical vision of God and the social order. For those who gathered at the Worker for worship, prayer was at the very center of their work and struggle. The dining area was cleaned before the service in the same way that the room was cleaned before serving meals. It remained as it was for the work—the life lived during the day. No separation was allowed or desired. Liturgy emerged and flowed with a committed life lived out in the world.

The year I lived at the Worker was one of the most difficult times of my life. Witnessing suffering close-up, without escape, and living in the context of poverty and destitution are not easy for a person from a middle-class background. I never became used to it nor was I good at attending to the suffering. The smells and horror of some lives I encountered have never left me. Nor has the essential lesson I learned at the Worker: the poor and destitute are no different from the affluent except in circumstance and opportunity. There is a thin line between hope and despair, affluence and poverty, well-being and destitution.

When the affluent pray, what do we pray for? Does the God who blesses us deny to the poor and destitute his blessing? Do the prayers of the poor counteract the prayers of the affluent? Are the affluent and the poor divided in life but united in God? Is salvation found in God or in the world? What is salvation? What does salvation mean here on earth? Are those in the soup line saved or condemned? Where do I stand in relation to God? When I sat in the basement with the men and women of the Bowery as they awaited their seat at the dinner table, these questions haunted me.

After receiving my doctorate a few years later, I embarked on a journey with the Maryknoll Fathers and traveled the world among the poor and the liberation theologians who speak for the poor. Here I encountered again the suffering of the poor and the worship of those on the outside of worldly power. In my travels I began to wonder whether the masses of poor and destitute people in Africa, Latin America, and Asia were so different from those of my dead in the Holocaust.

The echoes of Jewish life I found in these places were startling. I found a recovery of the Exodus and the prophetic tradition, even the Jewishness of Jesus. Here God was among the poor, or at least the theologians and the native people found him there. I wondered if God could be among the poor in the garbage dumps of Lima, Peru, but not among the Jews of Auschwitz. It could be that God is with both these Peruvians and the Jews. It could be that God is among neither peoples, then or now.

For many years I remained in this question of God's presence, as if the question itself was all-determining. Yet I was also called to form a religious practice, perhaps because of my personality and perhaps because of the circles I traveled in. I found myself an observer of religion and a participant at the same time. My place in both dimensions was unknown. Each was also deepening. I decided to form a discipline that allowed these two dimensions of my life to coexist. I did not know where it would lead. The decision was neither rational nor irrational. I was not able to articulate or even define what this discipline might be. I was traveling among others who were not my own. I also decided to travel to foreign territory within.

Like transporting oneself to a foreign country, the development of a discipline is dependent on the means of transportation available. For me the known vehicles were my own Jewish tradition and Asian spirituality, especially Zen Buddhism, which I was introduced to in my university days. Though known in learning, they were still foreign in the sense that visiting another country is different from reading about it.

When I was in my thirties, I began with Shabbat and Zen. On Friday nights I recited the Shabbat prayers. Each morning I sat in silence. The two practices are seemingly disparate. The first speaks of God's creation and the covenant at Sinai. The second seeks entry into the experience of nothingness. Still, both helped me enter the historical and internal landscape of the world in a different way. Questions remained. The colors of life changed.

I could not have embarked on Shabbat if I held to a rigorous honesty. And even today when my oldest child, Aaron, who shares the invocation of the Shabbat blessings, asks if I believe all that we read, I admit my limitation of belief. "Did God create the earth?" Aaron asked me some years ago. When I began a lecture on the complexity of the question he stopped me short. A simple yes or no would do. I told him that I was unsure.

Did God choose the Jews? Does God accompany us through history? In the service, I affirm that he does. In life, the answers elude me. Still, I continued in the service until the affirmation of truth became less important than the questions the words raised. After more than two decades of Shabbat observance, certain passages of the service continue to provoke me.

Is it right to thank God for choosing us and setting us apart as a people? What does "set apart" mean at a time when Jews are integrated into American life and often as not Christian friends share our Shabbat table? If Jews are set apart, can we also thank God for other times in history, the time of Auschwitz for example? Does our sense of being chosen also allow some Jews to act against non-Jews, Palestinians for example, in a manner that too closely resembles ways that others have acted against us?

For most people it is difficult to understand a religiosity that is unsure of itself or a faith shadowed by doubt and questions. Can a believer question the creation of the world as an act of God? Just as important is the question of God's presence in the world. Who after the Holocaust can be certain of this presence? Often it is said that faith is a gift and those without that gift must simply struggle along. Yet I find the biblical stories to be full of doubt. Many biblical stories seem without a clear destination. Some are difficult if not impossible to accept. Can I worship a God who tests Abraham's faith by his willingness to sacrifice Isaac? A God who judges the ancient Israelites' fidelity with a reign of death?

I entered faith through doubt. On Shabbat, past and present are in relation. Creation and chosenness are confronted by suffering and Holocaust. As I read the words of blessing I also have in mind Palestinians who experience these words as hypocrisy and worse. For Palestinians they are carriers of violence and exile.

Doubt can be a critical element of faith, relativizing all claims, including our own. Silence enters here, at least in my own evolving practice. Sitting quietly and regularly is an opening without claims or doubt. Shabbat is an assertion, albeit a beautiful one, and the questions that Shabbat raises for me are speculative no matter how deeply experienced. Zen seeks a reality beyond words and the presence of life without judgment or name.

To reach this point is a lifetime journey. Shabbat asserts a destiny. Zen silence refuses destination and destiny. To listen to what is inside of us and be attentive to what surrounds us, but not be captive to it, is a wonder. It is the practice of freedom. This freedom connects me to the world in a different way from Shabbat. Perhaps they work in tandem, as voices of self-correction and as postures in the world. One is with words, the other silent. One is with others, the other alone.

There are so many contradictions. Shabbat speaks of the end of exile. I experience Shabbat in affluence and security. Does the hope of ending exile speak to those on the other side of powers that often invoke religious symbols to legitimate atrocity?

Often I am asked about fidelity as I have come to understand it. What is fidelity? What or who are we faithful to? In an earlier time I responded that the call is to be faithful in and to history. Usually the people asking the question are religious in a more conventional sense. They *know* that fidelity is to God and that the ability to be faithful comes from God. Thus they see my definition of fidelity as a challenge or as a superficial response to a deeper question.

After the Holocaust, with faith in fragments, how can I affirm a sure anchor from which answers, power, and strength flow? How can I assert a God who is whole and holy when my experience is one of despair and waiting?

For Jews the Holocaust remains the ultimate shattering. My own sense is that a further shattering has occurred in response to the Holocaust in the formation and expansion of Israel. To many Jews the birth of Israel symbolizes a reformation of Jewish life. It asserts life where death reigned and holds open the possibility of the renewal of God's presence in the life of the people. And so it may be.

For me, the dispersion and oppression of the Palestinian people make this view impossible to hold. Empowerment is necessary to maintain one's integrity and survival. It can be the place from which a new interdependence can grow. When a nation is built on exclusivity and the disenfranchisement of others, then isolation and militarism are the norm. Ingathering can become another form of shattering. Jewish redemption from the Holocaust in the creation of Israel becomes a disaster for Palestinians. Has it become a disaster for Jews as well?

I remember well the recognition of injustice toward Palestinians and the further shattering it caused for me. It was during my junior year in college that I first traveled to Israel and encountered the injustice done to Palestinians. I had very little knowledge of Israel and even less about the Palestinians. In fact my curiosity about Israel came precisely because of this lack.

Years before, one of my Hebrew school teachers had extolled the virtues of Israel after his first visit there in 1968. As he spoke to me of Israel in glowing terms, I remembered a cover story in *Time* after the 1967 Arab-Israeli war. It featured Palestinians and their life after the war. An expulsion of Palestinians—one that had eerie parallels to their initial expulsion in 1948—had taken place and the occupation of the West Bank and Gaza was just beginning. I asked my teacher about Palestinians because I was curious to know if he had met any in Israel. When I mentioned Palestinians he flew into a rage and started shouting at me. I was quite naive at the time, without knowledge or ideology. I did not understand his anger. His fury forced me into a corner. When he shouted that I knew nothing of the situation because I had never been to Israel, I pledged that I would travel there if I ever had the chance.

In 1973, I was studying in London and had several travel breaks. I used one of them to travel to the Soviet Union. Another I used to travel to Israel. For one month I traveled the country and saw first-hand an inequality that was difficult for me to understand. People who looked like me, that is, Jews of European background, seemed like settlers on the land. They were building a modern country on the model of the United States. The native people, the Palestinians, seemed displaced and without focus. Within Israel they were a minority, citizens but decidedly second- or even third-class. On the West Bank, Palestinians were under occupation without citizenship. Israeli settlements were beginning to be built. All of this was pure observation. I asked myself why the Palestinians were under Jews and why equal citizenship was not a goal that Israel strove toward. I had never learned anything of substance about Israel in my decade of Hebrew school nor from the teacher whose anger spurred my journey. It was raw sensory data.

I returned in 1984 to give a lecture at Tantur, an ecumenical research center outside of Jerusalem. It was then that I first met Palestinians within and outside the borders of Israel. Soon tourism was replaced with conversation and travel to the sights of Palestinian life and the homes of Palestinian people. The exploration of Palestinian history startled me as did the arrogance of Jewish Israeli culture. I was supposed to feel at home in Israel, but instead I felt alien and alienated. Israeli society was too much like the segregated society I experienced in America. Instead of a movement toward integration and civil rights as was happening at home, however, the opposite was occurring in Israel. I witnessed a further hardening of the division between Jews and Palestinians, and another settler movement was underway in the West Bank and Gaza. This injustice could not be tolerated. I could not be silent. But with what words could I speak my dissent? Where would I find my voice?

As I began to break through the difficulties of worship and move beyond a paralysis that needed assent before ritual, the most important holiday of the Jewish year, Passover, became impossible for me. How can I celebrate our liberation when another people is enslaved? If applied to the entire world the celebration would never be possible. Here was a most specific case of direct Jewish responsibility, but it was being evaded. Our fervent desire for liberation after the Holocaust was being perverted in the oppression of another people.

Paralysis of belief is different from what I experience in my waning energy to celebrate Passover. Passover is impossible for me because the contradictions of real oppression are too great. It is precisely the vantage point of the other, the Palestinians, that brought Passover to an end.

Can fidelity be seen as a movement within and beyond the historical? As a place from which to judge history in a critical manner? Shabbat and Zen make it possible to look at Passover and judge the community's assertion of liberation at the expense of another people's oppression. The critical examination of Passover as liberation in our time becomes more articulate by exploring an internal affirmation of spirituality.

Here again resolution is elusive. Contradiction is present. The perceived necessity of choosing Shabbat over Passover, for example, can be turned on its head. Why not celebrate both or abandon both as a point of consistency? Is one holy day exempt from critique while another deepens it?

Perhaps this is simply another aspect of the fragments of Jewish life after the Holocaust and Israel. Each Jew pieces life together in a particular and eclectic way. She crosses boundaries that often intersect like an unplanned tapestry. The contours of that tapestry are uneven.

When Jews and those from different faith traditions who are also experiencing fragmentation are together, a sensibility emerges beyond the individual. One encounters a diaspora sensibility in more than a geographic sense or even the traditional Jewish sense of commonality within diversity. The diaspora encountered is a place where the fragments of different traditions and lives come together in new ways. There is a particularity found among Jews in this new diaspora and a particularity that is evolving among the various other peoples found in the diaspora. Jews, then, form a particular aspect of a larger community that is forming around the conditions of exile and fragmentation experienced by many peoples. Thus Jewish particularity in this evolving diaspora is in dialogue with two foundational realities. One is the Jewish world from which I come. The other is the broader community I find myself within.

I have found this to be true in my own life. It is almost as if I am traveling the diaspora, carrying my heritage and history and encountering other heritages and histories. The interaction is one of solidarity and confrontation. I am forced to expand my capacity for belief and action. I also become more focused on the interior life that is formed and unformed, affirmed and challenged in these encounters. Piecing together a post-Holocaust Jewish life is never static. Traveling the diaspora is a spiritual vocation.

Over time, one experiences the need for an anchor, or so it seems in my life. Exploring fragmentation can lead to subsequent levels of fragmentation until the experience of fragmentation becomes foundational itself. A foundation of fragmentation is quite different from a foundation that is fragmenting. The former has a place of origin from which it has been expelled, and it involves a desire to find meaning even if the original foundation is no longer accessible. The latter ultimately loses the possibility of depth as the resources from which it comes recede into the distance. The danger is that fragmentation becomes less a search for wholeness and more an experience that has few resources for continuing on the journey.

At some point the resources of tradition become inaccessible. The quest for depth reaches a dead end. The exiles refuse to continue on the journey. Either their inability to see a journey or a destiny at all becomes overriding or, in fear, they attempt to re-embrace the foundational reality as if the shattering had not occurred.

What allows movement forward? What propels the continuation of the journey into the unknown? What helps sustain the courage to continue to piece together the fragments after the Holocaust *and* Israel? What strengthens Jews to travel the diaspora without fear of losing their own identity or even the possibility of further shattering an already fragmented identity?

I look back at the difficulties I have with worship and the subsequent creation of an admittedly eclectic discipline. What has been with me since the beginning? What is the main thread, the continuity that underlies my journey? The covenant. Not a whole covenant without question and doubt. Or even a covenant that can be named or found within one tradition. This covenant has accompanied me even as I searched for it.

I almost missed the naming of the covenant. One night after a lecture at a state university in Maryland, I was taken out to eat by Gersham Nelson who had invited me to speak. Nelson was the chair of the religion department and a native of the Caribbean. The conference was on the 500th anniversary of Columbus's "discovery" of the Americas. My lecture was interesting because of the audience response. I was used to critiquing religiosity in front of religious people who attended my lectures, but about midway through I realized that the audience was largely secular. They were nodding their heads in complete agreement because, for most, religion was outmoded and prejudiced. I reversed course in the middle and a lively discussion ensued.

According to Nelson, I confused my listeners because I started my lecture in midstream. Indeed he had experienced this in reading several of my books. I asked if he could clarify what he meant by this. "You begin in the middle and move forward," Nelson began, "but you don't announce your prior assumptions, the foundation that your conclusions emerge from." When I asked for further clarification and a concrete example of the unannounced foundation, he replied simply: "The covenant."

Though I have become more articulate about the covenant and its place in my life, I question where this covenant comes from. Where does it reside? By what name is it to be called? On Shabbat I find it within the Jewish tradition. When I sit Zen I find the covenant within silence. In Peru among the poor, I experience the covenant when God is called on to empower the people. When I think of the Catholic Worker movement, the covenant is palpable. In pictures I have seen of Jesus in breadlines among the poor, the covenant is invoked with an intensity that is haunting. Do I embrace the Jesus portrayed as a Christian? Or do I embrace the Jesus of the breadlines as a Jew?

Traveling the diaspora, the covenant takes center stage as an almost undefinable yet intimate reality. At moments it is close to me. Often it is just beyond me. It is the revealed covenant of the Bible. Yet it evolves independent of its original revelation. For me the covenant is wherever people grapple with history at its deepest level. The covenant embodies the questions and tensions of personal and communal life. It is not a place of rest. It is a calling forth.

The covenant is multifaceted. It is experienced in different ways when approached from various perspectives. Shabbat and Zen become two vantage points of fragmentation and integration on the same path. The motion is forward. Both point beyond themselves and transcend their own particularity. Here the answer is less important than the experience. Truth ceases to be a primary objective. Does the covenant propose a truth? Or is it an accompanying inner voice without destination or destiny? Perhaps the destiny is found within the path itself. In the covenant, endings are beginnings. The discipline of searching and seeking to embrace the covenant is itself of value.

Perhaps the fragmentation of so many traditions is itself a call forward. So often during Shabbat and sitting in silence I feel a gratitude that comes from the possibility afforded by the brokenness of tradition. How else will I experience this diaspora and the beauty within it? How else will my fidelity be tested and strengthened? The suffering that has brought about the fragmentation I inherit is beyond words. It continues today in many countries and cultures. Still, within the horror, the journey continues.

The covenant beckons and fidelity is called for. I often wonder if it is possible to be grateful for a journey that is uneven, discontinuous, even violent. And yet the theoretical question is belied by the experience. It is precisely in the brokenness that gratitude comes into view. I experience a power that sometimes overwhelms me. Sometimes the power is so subtle that I miss the experience. I often miss the overwhelming and subtle experience of gratitude because I seek to place it within a framework that no longer exists. I seek to place a reality that is beyond naming into a historical naming, or I mistake a historical naming for my own vocabulary. I search for order and certainty and replace the possibilities inherent in a dynamic experience that elicits names but eludes a final naming.

It may be that the world has always been fragmented beyond the order imposed upon it by human beings. Perhaps the covenant has always traveled freely and been embraced by those searching beyond the confines of the known. The mystical path is found in every tradition and is testimony to this search. But the reality I experience is beyond the esoteric and the few. The fragmentation and the search are found within ordinary life among the many. It is at the very heart of evolving disciplines of spirituality and everyday life. It is not beyond intact traditions. It is within traditions fragmented by history.

✺

To TRAVEL THE DIASPORA is to enter into other evolving sensibilities and connections to history. It is a move forward and backward, embracing diversity in the present and past, often at the same time. The struggle to be faithful is found in many places today; the same struggle can be found historically. If fidelity cannot be confined in the contemporary world to any one place or community, this has to be true for the past as well. The struggle to be faithful is nourished in this two-fold movement. The terrain of embrace and the resources of nourishment are expanded.

My fidelity is informed by Jews and others struggling in the present. I think here of Ari Shavit, a Jewish-Israeli journalist who protests Israeli power when it abuses Palestinians. And Sara Roy, a child of Holocaust survivors, who travels among Palestinians and is a world expert on the economy of Gaza. I am also nourished by the witness of Archbishop Oscar Romero, who stood with the poor of El Salvador and was murdered for speaking on their behalf. And Gustavo Gutiérrez, who lives with the poor of his native Peru and embodies the theology of liberation, which speaks of a God active in the liberation of the marginalized and dispossessed. So, too, with history. I am nourished by the German-Jewish philosopher Franz Rosenzweig and the German Christian Dietrich Bonhoeffer, who resisted Hitler. Further back in history I am nourished by the founders of the great religions, including Buddha and Jesus.

Should I be denied their insights and struggle? Should I deny the resources that are available to me and carried by others in the new diaspora? By denying them I diminish my own sensitivity to others around me. I diminish my own struggle to be faithful. Since in so many ways those who struggle to be faithful are connected through borrowings, mutual influence, and common trajectories, my denial would be a denigration of their contributions to our common history.

The broader tradition of faith and struggle can be found in the imagining of a diaspora that is continuous over time. It is part of a search through history for justice and love, which, though always incomplete even in its depth, is somehow complete in its effort. Buddha, Jesus, Rosenzweig, Bonhoeffer, Shavit, and Romero all sought commitment and community. In this search, the covenant is present, and the particular language of their search, whether theological, philosophical, or secular, sheds light on the struggles of our own day. I see this light when I take my place in the calling of a broader tradition. Here I find provisions for my journey.

2
Dream Gathering
in Jerusalem

IN 1988, AT THE HEIGHT of the first Palestinian uprising, I had a peculiar and startling dream. It remains vivid to this day.

In the dream, the most prominent Jewish intellectuals and religious leaders of our century were brought to Israel to share their ideas about the crisis facing Israel. One by one each testified in front of a distinguished panel of judges. The judges were the prime ministers of Israel since its inception in 1948.

This crisis was multifaceted. In December 1987, several Palestinians in the occupied Gaza Strip were murdered by Israeli soldiers. Demonstrations immediately broke out and soon the unrest had spread to the West Bank and Jerusalem. Over the next months many Palestinians were arrested, injured, and killed. Widespread rioting was followed by an announced Israeli policy of might and beatings. Indiscriminate beatings and the breaking of bones were reported and shown on the nightly news in America and around the world. The coverage was vivid; the violence of the Israeli response was caught on camera. In America, Jewish viewers of this violence were caught off guard.

To see Jewish soldiers beat unarmed civilians demonstrating for their rights to self-determination and the end of occupation reversed the image of Israelis fighting only in self-defense. The sense of Jewish innocence and Palestinian terrorism was turned inside out. The Israeli response could not be seen as self-defense. Jewish dissent against the policies of occupation could now be heard and this too was reported in print and on television. It was almost as if a war complementary to the one between Jews and Palestinians was breaking out among Jews in Israel and America. A civil war of words and anguish between Jews was on the horizon. Thus it became a defining point for Israel and others. There was a collective sense of having reached a turning point in Jewish history.

In my dream Hannah Arendt, Judah Magnes, Martin Buber, Gershom Scholem, and Albert Einstein testified before these legendary leaders. The founder of Israel, David Ben-Gurion, was there, as was the irascible Golda Meir. The tough countenances of Yitzhak Shamir and Yitzhak Rabin were in full view. Contemporary Jewish intellectuals were also invited. The roll call was formidable. Abraham Heschel, Bernard Lewis, Michael Walzer, and Noam Chomsky all testified. I was also invited. I would be the last to testify.

The room was large. In the middle of the room was a conference table where the prime ministers sat. At the head of the table was a chair for the person testifying. The room was enclosed in glass. Looking out you could see the barren desert hills that surround Jerusalem. If someone looked toward the room from the outside, everyone was clearly visible. The witnesses were vulnerable to the power of the assembled ministers. They were also vulnerable to the world outside. The dramatic setting complemented the dramatic meeting. We were there to chart the future of the Jewish people.

After each testimony, the ministers left together and the witness stayed in the room until the ministers rendered their judgment. Then the witness left the room and continued on his or her journey.

Each witness testified alone. None were privy to the testimony of the others nor the subsequent judgment. When my turn came I was nervous. After an initial nervousness, I shared what I had been thinking and writing for some years. "The challenge for the Jewish people, indeed the future of the Jewish people, lies in a solidarity with those whom we had displaced, the Palestinian people," I testified. I advised a confession of our wrongs and an immediate invitation to Yassir Arafat to meet with the present prime minister in Jerusalem. There a new history would begin, emphasizing repentance, equality, justice, and mutual respect.

The panel listened attentively, betraying no emotion or judgment. Then they adjourned. Some minutes later as I was looking out of the windows at the desert hills, an Israeli military guard entered the room. He approached and told me that the prime ministers had concluded their deliberations. The guard pulled out his revolver, placed it at my temple, and pulled the trigger. At that moment I awoke from my dream. I was perspiring but felt strangely at peace. I had done what I had to do. As it turned out, the gun was not loaded. I had survived. I was alive.

I have thought about the meaning of this dream often. What remains years later are the issues the dream raises. Primary among them is the fact that the future of the Jewish people is being decided at this moment in history.

I feel that the crisis is more than ephemeral and strategic. In my own lifetime, Jewish history has been radically changed by the empowerment of Israel and the legitimation of that empowerment by Jewish leadership in Israel and America. A corollary to these significant facts is that Jewish leaders have an incredible responsibility in light of this decisive moment. If Israel, like any state, has a certain logic about it with regard to power, then the role of the intellectual and religious leadership to legitimize or call that power to account is decisive.

For most of our history, Jewish intellectuals, and, by extension, religious thinkers and activists, have operated outside a state framework or, especially since the Enlightenment period, within states where Jews are a marginal and sometimes despised minority. Some of these leaders were advisors to power, others acted as representatives of the Jewish people. Most have been keenly aware that their own survival and that of our people was at stake. Even the criticism of unjust power was addressed on the margins. If this criticism threatened power, the result was a larger social and political upheaval that Jews were involved in, but did not control.

An advisor to or critic of power has certain limitations and certain freedoms, especially when the power is not one's own and the history, past and future, is of another people and state. Though not without consequences for Jews, the role of Jewish leaders was heightened considerably with the establishment of Israel. Israel is important in Jewish history for many reasons, but the fundamental one is independence. This involves the task of charting, for the first time in two thousand years, a Jewish destiny in Jewish hands.

≈

WHAT WE HAVE DONE with this responsibility is difficult to assess. Israel has existed for little more than half a century. It was formed only four years before my birth. I have grown up with Israel. We are living coterminously with its origins.

Still, the images that were presented to me in Hebrew school—the tilling of the desert, the heroic freedom fighters, a place for survivors of the Holocaust, the struggle for a new Jewish commonwealth of social and economic equality—have all been tarnished. The Israeli victory in the 1967 Arab-Israeli War led to decades of occupation and settlement. The "miracle" of victory is a nightmare of displacement for Palestinians and an internal division among Jews.

The 1948 war that established Israel as a nation demands reflection rather than celebration. Palestinian witnesses and historians have asserted from the beginning what Jewish historians now confirm. The creation of an independent Jewish state depended on the removal of hundreds of thousands of Palestinians from what became Israel. Few Jews in America are aware of this. I certainly never learned this history from any Jewish source in my childhood or beyond.

The embrace of one's history is more difficult after its complexities have been uncovered. For Jews reconciling the vision of Israel with its beginnings and its unfolding is more and more difficult. That is why where once there was a ferocious cry on Israel's behalf when criticism was raised, today there is an eerie silence. Even the fiftieth anniversary celebrations of Israeli independence in 1998 were muted. Some were even abandoned.

On the threshold of the twenty-first century, this culpability and silence threatens to become permanent. Anyone who travels in Israel among Palestinians knows that Palestine has been destroyed. Millions of Palestinian refugees remain outside their homeland. The map of Israel as it exists in the twenty-first century shows an expanded state that stretches from Tel Aviv to the Jordan River.

What is left of Palestine is surrounded on both sides by Israel. Internally, Palestine is segmented by Jewish settlements, settlers, and security zones. Externally, it is surrounded by security zones and settlements. In effect, the remnant Palestinians of 1948 within Israel, numbering more than a million people, are now joined by a second remnant Palestinian population in Jerusalem and the West Bank, more than two million people. The deliberate underdevelopment of the occupied territories for more than three decades of occupation has taken its toll. So too has the rate of expropriation of territory.

In my journeys to Israel and Palestine over the years, I have seen the landscape of Palestine changed almost beyond recognition. The expansion of Jerusalem and the settlements are the most obvious pieces of this terrible development. I remember quite well the building of Jewish housing to surround Jerusalem and the transformation of the older part of the city from a Palestinian area to a religiously devout Jewish community. The sealing of the borders of Israel and Palestine divides Jews and Palestinians. It only makes more difficult the confession and action needed for justice and reconciliation. Palestinian refugee status now appears to be permanent.

In the formation of Jewish identity in the West, Israel's presence is changing. It is becoming a silent rather than vocal partner. This is quite different from when I was young. Then, Israel was touted as a source of pride and purity. At Hillel centers in universities across the country, Israel is simply assumed as fundamental to Jewish identity. The details of Israel's formation and existence are unexplored. These details are too difficult to raise without challenging the identity that rabbis and other Jewish leaders attempt to inculcate in university-educated Jews.

Hence the "truth" squads I have experienced over the years as a public speaker. These are students trained to confront "anti-Israel" speakers on campus. I find they become silent when those who are deemed to be anti-Israel speak in a complex and moving way about the future of the Jewish people. The hope of overcoming sealed borders and moving toward a just and equal reconciliation with the Palestinian people surprises these students and sometimes moves them.

These Jewish students, the young ones and the many who are not so young, are met along the way in their search, or what can become a search, if the deepest yearnings of a person and a Jew are spoken to. Often one sees the question before Jews begging to be asked—the question of how to respond to our need for confession and reconciliation with the Palestinian people—and often this question is unasked. It is definitive by its very absence. With the assertion of a militant persona, the "tough" Jew overrides the entire Jewish tradition to confront those who speak the truth. In my experience, however, this tough Jew is a Jew on the brink of being lost and betraying a history of suffering and hope. By defending injustice and silence, tough Jews empty the future of possibility. Those who refuse this toughness are left to wander alone.

The question remains. Tough Jews are unable to confront truth. They hide behind a banner that disguises injustice. Those defined as "weak" are often distant from the community and find their solace and solidarity elsewhere. Why not? Tough Jews have assumed ownership of the tradition and Jewish identity, or so it seems. The future seems torn between the tough and the weak. Many in the middle go through the motions or walk away. I encounter many of these Jews. They long for peace and a path that leads toward justice. Often they are met with silence or anger. When identity becomes a battleground, even the places of comfort and dissent atrophy.

What of those involved in Jewish renewal, the followers of Arthur Waskow and Michael Lerner, or even Jewish feminists like Judith Plaskow, justice-seeking Jews who integrate traditional Judaism and modern sensibilities? I have met them as well. They attempt to create a new Jewish establishment. Yet the argument they make for peace between Jews and Palestinians is often patronizing. I find the space for reconciliation with justice to be limited. It is almost as if the argument for peace with Palestinians, once made, becomes one among other issues for Jews. As time moves on, the issue itself is bypassed.

The new Jewish mysticism and politics of meaning tend to make peripheral the injustice that continues. We celebrate God, wholeness, and inclusion. New meanings are ascribed to the Sabbath ritual and the moon is reincorporated into the Jewish calendar. Even peace marches in Jerusalem and elsewhere attest to the wholeness of Jewish renewal.

To compete with tough Jews in the center and on the right, they become tough Jews on the left. Again, thought is limited, but in a different way.

What could be better than to incorporate into this renewal contemporary Jewish worship, feminism, and activism? A full Jewish life is achieved within and articulated to those outside. As it turns out, it is perfectly possible to celebrate one's Jewishness while another people is displaced and living in segregated and "autonomous" areas.

What I find missing is justice, not simply for a year or a decade, or even the sixth decade, but in the possibility that the displacement of the Palestinian people is now permanent. This permanent displacement continues during times of war *and* during a peace process. It is celebrated by the Jewish world, as the aftermath of the 1967 war and the 1993 Oslo agreements testify. When a permanent displacement takes place within the context of celebration then a serious flaw in reflection and commitment is exposed. If our sense of Jewishness is dependent on a victory that consigns millions to wandering and to exile, then one wonders what the future content of Jewish life will be. This is a collective *and* personal challenge.

The fight against assimilation is prominent in Jewish discussions and typically involves the question of intermarriage. Yet it is a chimera if we have already assimilated to power, to the state, and to victories that involve the creation of a permanent refugee population. What is distinctiveness? Marrying within our community as our actions mirror the actions of any other community?

Renewal and injustice are silently joined. And yet the accusing images of silence and complicity remain. They surround us without being noticed, and when images appear, they startle us. As the years progress, will the ability to speak and act for justice remain? If the demand for justice is buried for generations, will the very vocabulary of justice atrophy? If the question of justice is silenced, what basis is there for Jewish life? When I speak for justice in other parts of the world I feel like a hypocrite. Can I argue for justice for South Africans and Bosnians and not seek justice for Palestinians?

It is not just Israel. Jewish upward mobility in America has also taken a toll. In politics, business, and the academy, Jews and Jewishness are celebrated in a way that was unimaginable when I was growing up in the 1950s and 1960s. Making it in America has been important but, as with Israel, the cost continues to be high. Jews are now respectable and sought after. Yet there is a cost to respectability. Can Jews fulfill the ethical demands of justice in the United States when we are called upon to buttress, advise, and manage a political and economic system whose global impact is morally ambiguous and often destructive?

Here too renewal is joined with injustice. When the demands of justice are bracketed, religion is personalized and abstracted from the world. Like the Christians we often criticize, we, too, can dance in the street as the world burns.

Within the assimilation to power and the state in Israel and America, a new Jewish exile has formed. How often I encounter these exiles from Jewish institutions and houses of prayer! Jews in exile often feel that they are the only Jews in this situation. My experience is that one is actually many. I encounter these "only" Jews in movements against injustice, including movements of solidarity with Palestinians. Most of these Jews are American and European. Some of them are Israelis in Israel. A large percentage of these Israeli Jews now live in America. The return to the land of our origin has produced its own exile.

These exiles join others in a new global diaspora forming in our time. People from all religions and ideologies find themselves outside of the cultures and communities they were born within. The movement from exile to diaspora is significant. Diaspora is dispersion. It also demands the formation of community and the fusion of ideals and values into new configurations. In the diaspora, a condition of exile becomes an opportunity. The pain of exile can become a difficult affirmation. Over time, exiles who are "others" begin to recognize a common plight and possibility. A shared despair about the world and our own people becomes a shared hope to forge a different world for our children. The diaspora is a fusing of necessity and opportunity where despair becomes hope, and fear, courage.

Perhaps this is what my dream was actually about, the last hope to speak to my own people and to begin with others to turn toward justice and reconciliation in a world of violence and atrocity. My testimony was an attempt to avoid the diminution of the Jewish tradition, perhaps its end, at least as we have known and inherited it. The ability to speak truth to power is already a witness to this diaspora. For where will the support continue to come from? Here values within the Jewish tradition, strained and atrophying under the assault of injustice and the state, are fused with support and values coming from others suffering a similar assault within their own traditions and cultures.

It was naive of me to think that Israel would respond differently to my critique than any other nation would. Does moral persuasion override the imperatives of power? Are presidents and prime ministers guided by traditions and values that challenge power and give priority to the suffering of the displaced and the poor? Few political leaders make decisions as if everything is at stake. For me an entire history of suffering and struggle, an ethical base from which to judge the world and establish the possibility of harmony within and among peoples, is on the line.

In the dream the gun is pointed and fired. The chamber is empty. When I fall to the ground a profound silence surrounds me. What next? To seek the prime ministers for another round of discussions? Perhaps. To seek other intellectuals and religious leaders to testify as I did? At times.

The dream leads elsewhere. "Leave this house and begin again," the dream prophesies. "Go with those who will walk with you. Pursue a way of life that responds to the times in which we live."

When I awoke from my dream, I walked away from a confinement of conscience. I walked toward a life that refuses complicity and renewal. Where the dream leaves off, life begins. The exile begins. The "other" ceases to be other. We ask each other what we have learned and what we can share. The diaspora emerges amid the ruins of traditions and peoples. A new discipline is fashioned from the discarded, the forgotten, and the foreign.

Defeat, then, is imbued with another sensibility. The tragic is acknowledged as a quiet strength evolves. How often that strength seems beyond us and out of reach! When joined with others it becomes a testimony to a future of justice and peace. That testimony becomes a chorus that one day becomes so beautiful and compelling that even presidents and prime ministers heed its voice.

Is this what the empty gun illustrates? That though injustice continues on its way and the hour is very late, there is still time? What will happen when the time does come, I do not know.

The dream that startles us also turns us around. It encourages me to give everything to the world.

3
Practicing Exile

As the diaspora awaits its formation, the exile continues. Many Jews are unaware of this exile. Long ago they disassociated themselves from the Jewish people and buried this wound in other pursuits. Others feel the exile directly as a loneliness and a burden.

Jews in exile are deprived of ordinary community life because they refuse to accept the "normality" that hides a system of displacement and injustice. The exile is powerless to change this normalization and cannot except it either. I understand the situation because I experience it daily. It is like being caught in a dream where words fall on deaf ears and drift away into nothingness.

Some people counsel patience and confirm the importance of the exile's witness. Others see the exile as bothersome and destructive. Often the exile irritates those who are supportive and is punished by those she opposes. For what reason do we continue on in this quest?

Jewish exiles have little to support them. Liberal thinkers and progressive political actors from other communities, especially the white Christian community, have other issues and concerns. Jews were important to them in the 1950s and 1960s. As long-sufferers with canonical texts held in common, the rediscovery of the beauty of Judaism and Jewishness opened Christians to another way of embracing their own faith. Christianity could jettison its history of bigotry and atrocity and embark on a new era. The shift from a demonized Jewry to a romanticized Jewry allowed this renewal. Now other issues and peoples dominate their attention. Our empowerment has rendered us too complex. We are neither demons nor angels. It is more difficult to define and place us in a useful category.

For Palestinians, this means a peripheral status in this discourse. To be in solidarity with Palestinians is only to confuse the issue of solidarity with Jews. Why court, and in a negative way, the interest of the Jewish establishment? Why brush up against the charge of being anti-Jewish? I have experienced this fear often. It is strange to have adults with stature and security fall silent in the face of a charge of anti-Semitism. Some Christian leaders of the ecumenical dialogue privately admit fearing this charge leveled against them.

Since Christians no longer have a need for Jews, why should they stand up for Jewish dissidents? How could this possibly add to their prestige or influence? Many of the issues that concern progressive Christians, from critique of militarism and support of African American empowerment to feminism, have opened space for the marginalized. Indeed many have made a career of speaking to these issues. Why jeopardize this achievement for Jewish dissidents?

In the forming diaspora, Jews retain a special quality. On the material side, Jews are relatively affluent. Few Jewish dissenters miss meals or live in substandard housing. Few suffer discrimination within the context of a communal prejudice or cross borders to escape injustice, human-rights violations, or war. They are almost invisible because of relative affluence.

I often hear Jews in exile ponder the worthiness of our cause. How can a Jew in exile compare situations with an African American struggling to overcome racism, with a Salvadoran who flees decades of civil war, or with a Palestinian who flees Jewish power? Each exile is clearly different in content and scope. It remains an issue, however, when Jews on the margins rightly protest their exclusion. Are we not also struggling within our context? How is this argued and justified?

Sometimes Christians rebuild their heritage by using other peoples for renewal. Among the oppressed, fending off the next supplicant to ensure your place at the table is a fact of life. Human nature remains in movements for social justice.

I wonder what it is to build an empire—even a small one, but yours nonetheless—when your own people are struggling and things are becoming worse for the majority. I think here of some African Americans and feminists in the political, business, and academic worlds who are upwardly mobile while their community continues to struggle.

Achievement and strength are necessary and part of the road to empowerment. As a Jew I know this. But when it becomes clear that only you and a very few like you will make it, that great numbers of your own people are encountering still greater difficulties, what does one do? When do the words of justice become empty despite the applause and the accolades for one's bravery in speaking truth to power? At some point speaking truth to power can become one's vehicle of assimilation *to* power.

Perhaps a dialectical relationship between those who speak for the powerless and those whose misery continues is an unresolvable element of life and society. It is difficult for me to speak boldly to the contradictions found here. The case of Jewish suffering in Europe has been told so often and memorialized so frequently, *as if Jews in the present are suffering,* that the charge against others of using suffering as a lever for advancement is mute.

Jewish status in the West has advanced in proportion to the establishment and promotion of a narrative that features the Holocaust as central to Jewish memory and experience. That narrative also functions to protect Jewish advancement in America and Israel from the type of criticism generally applied to other communities and nations. The use of suffering as a way of empowerment has, at least in the Jewish case, precipitated the Palestinian diaspora *and* the Jewish exile. Paradoxically, the use of suffering as a way toward empowerment strikes Jews in exile twice: as the reason for exile from the Jewish people and the distance from others who are in exile.

For what Jew, conscious of contemporary political and economic reality, can assert suffering as the central problematic of Jewish life? My experience is that few among the suffering today find the assertion of past Jewish suffering to be a lesson that they need to be constantly reminded of. I agree with them.

My analysis of Jewish exile may seem like another, albeit covert, attempt to prove the uniqueness of Jewish experience. Jews remain unique whether in suffering, in empowerment, in exile within empowerment, or in exile within the new diaspora. Caution is crucial here. An analytical rather than a mystical interpretation of the situation needs to be maintained.

The distinction that the literary and political critic Edward Said makes between "religious" and "secular" criticism is important. The religious tends to bend reality to its own preconceptions, absolutize them, and present these understandings as reality itself. The secular does just the opposite: it investigates, is open to further questions, and is brutally honest in viewing the complications and contradictions of any situation. As a Palestinian, Said knows the exile well.

The Jewish understanding of uniqueness is found in the religious terminology of chosenness. It is central to Jewish discourse over the millennia. When we are with other Jews it is easy to assume this category and apply it against both the Jewish community and those who speak on behalf of others. I assert this chosenness daily in prayer and Shabbat. It can become a claim of a more profound, even predestined, exile.

It is hard to deny that central themes in the tradition find their way into contemporary feeling and analysis. Regardless of how it is interpreted and how dependent the secular analysis is on religious themes, the need for expression remains. As a Jew, I can learn from how others see their own exile, but in the end, Jews are formed within a particular history with particular symbols and themes. While the peculiar understandings of exile that Jews have cannot and should not become normative for others, to relinquish these understandings only encourages a further estrangement and loneliness. As a Jew, I need to come to terms with chosenness rather than distance myself from it.

I enter a terrible dilemma. To speak of exile in affluence and security is not only strange to those who are materially suffering. It counters the entire movement of the Jewish people to "overcome" suffering and displacement through empowerment. The very suggestion of a new exile is startling and carries connotations of relinquishing power and reverting again to a place of weakness. So is the exile's warning that Jews are likely to find themselves on the periphery of the new diaspora. To many observers, this risk seems ridiculous and threatening. Perhaps it is. If I seek to trade individual prosperity for my peoples' suffering then my claim is hypocritical. I espouse a lie that disguises personal ambition. It is better that the Jewish people are empowered than those in exile be celebrated. Especially after this bitter history of suffering, Jews in exile cannot seek a situation of powerlessness for the community. Yet to cease asking whether there is not an alternative to being victim or oppressor is somehow to abandon my Jewishness.

What is a Jew to do then? I would be foolish to expose the contradictions of Jews as the Warsaw ghetto was created and sealed. But I find it impossible to remain silent as those who claim to be heirs of the Holocaust displace another people in the name of the Jewish victims of the Holocaust. This is why a strictly secular interpretation of exile seems impossible to me. Or rather, Said's interpretation of the secular—as open, rigorous, able to deal with complexity, and yet at the same time committed—seems absolutely essential to a religious understanding of exile. I enter exile as a choice because this secular sensibility critiques a contemporary Jewish religiosity that legitimates or is silent in the face of the unjust policies of Israel and America. The details force the issue: the homecoming that renders people homeless, the settling of the land that unsettles another people.

This is the beginning of the journey toward exile. Since overt religious and ideological language posits the dream without the details, the only language to speak, at least for most Jews, is a secular language of protest. The authentic Jewish religious language of our time is framed by details and protest. It calls the community from injustice to justice and from exclusion to inclusion. Secular language carries the Jewish tradition forward because traditional language is infected with displacement and atrocity.

How often I encounter "secular" Jews carrying the values of the Jewish tradition with them. Only one image, a recurring and religious image, comes into view. I see a long line of "only" and often "secular" Jews carrying the covenant into exile with them.

WHAT WILL SUSTAIN US in this journey? How do we keep the focus on the long run of history when so many complications face us on a daily basis? How can we maintain our fidelity when the Jewish community is of little support and the wider community is preoccupied with other "issues"? How do we keep from being sidetracked into a renewal that is comfortable in its identity and able to compartmentalize issues until the central issue of our time is relativized?

Perhaps the answer is in the practice of exile itself. For me the practice of exile involves the secular and religious, for while the exile is obvious and can be analyzed by those who seek to understand it, it is also hidden in those who face the travails of exile. The public and private are the two faces of exile. In the public realm a certain rigor and focus is necessary because opposition is constant and character assassination is frequent. The years of aloneness are also demanding. In private there is no audience and public assaults carry a special poignancy when the crowd disperses.

Who is there in these moments? Who is with us when futility of action is obvious? When one is derided or worse, pronounced a prophet and then sent on her way? Who is there to soften the exile? To lend it meaning? To encourage our fidelity?

What reason is there to enter exile when others explain away the tragedy that is depriving Jewish history of its moral and ethical center? One reason is that the practice of exile is the attempt to be faithful, faithful to a history and the suffering within it; to a God of history found in the ancient covenant and rediscovered in affirmation and debate by each generation of Jews.

Fidelity poses further questions. Can I speak of a God of history in the midst of oppression, affluence, and complicity? Does God bless injustice, displacement, and torture? Is this God found in exile? In the practice of exile does a different God appear? One that is with me in the speaking and acting upon the truths I come to know? Is it possible that the God found within the practice of exile is awaiting a new language in order to be spoken of?

A tension emerges between solitude and solidarity. The practice of exile is walking with the public and private aloneness that is part of the struggle to be faithful. It must be balanced with solidarity, especially with those on the other side of Jewish power. The tension I find most difficult is avoiding a false resolution, as if solitude precludes solidarity or solidarity overcomes solitude. For solidarity does not allow me to transcend my situation or make me into someone else, a Palestinian for example. It does not allow a false transcendence or symmetry with those deprived of a homeland and freedom.

In solitude I grapple with who I am, and become more deeply aware of the commitments and complexities of my own being. Solidarity is tempered by this awareness. I may be welcomed by others, but the fight for freedom is the struggle of the oppressed. Even if the solitude of a Jew in exile is characterized by reflection and depth in relation to Jewish history, Jewish solidarity with others is limited in its claims and work. I find no way out of this tension of solitude and solidarity. Solidarity without solitude or solitude without solidarity is false. To resolve this tension is to falsify the predicament of Jews and others.

The tension between solitude and solidarity does not essentialize the Jewish experience. In traveling the diaspora, I have become aware that the capacity for solitude and solidarity is within all peoples and is highlighted by personality, history, culture, and tradition. At certain times, the tension becomes a paralysis or a false identification. At other times, the tension becomes a forceful and creative expression of fidelity. The mixture of depression and expression, poetry and activism, the speaking of truth and the acting upon it, is part of the solitude and solidarity that characterizes the practice of exile. If the practice of exile is the end of innocence about my own people, it must be the end of innocence about all peoples, including those whom I embrace in solidarity.

With the end of innocence comes the hope for redemption. Solidarity embraced is less an answer or a goal, for the achieved goal itself presents new challenges. *In exile I realize that solidarity forces another level of solitude, an aloneness that I never overcome even as it becomes an avenue for introspection and love.* Redemption is always ahead of me, a tantalizing possibility that when described in detail or announced as having arrived, seems false. It is a gloss on reality rather than a grappling with it. What I seek is to be redeemed from is the struggle to be faithful. The tension of solitude and solidarity is a burden. It also gives rise to my fidelity.

Do I seek a God who redeems me from this tragic and beautiful tension? As if God will release me from the struggle itself or resolve the struggle on terms above and beyond the human? The God I find in exile is a God who is with me in my solitude *and* solidarity. It is a God who is present where I am.

In the displacement, torture, and murder of Palestinians, in the sealing of the borders that makes permanent loss and exclusion, the center of Jewish history has been turned inside out and gutted. A Jew in exile knows this at the deepest level of his being. The attempt to renew that history is a return to a false innocence and redemption contradicted by the details of history. Solidarity with the Palestinian people cannot restore that history as though we can move back in time. Nor can solidarity transcend this history, as though a new social order absolves us of past mistakes.

Solidarity recognizes that Jewish history *as we have known and in-herited it* is over. Those in exile embody this ending. But they also point toward and embody a new history and identity that one day will come into being.

It is the exile's plight that this future will be experienced by others in another time and in a configuration as yet unknown. Jews in exile today only experience the end. This adds to our burden. How diffi-cult it is to testify to an end without at least experiencing a taste of the future!

⋘

THE EXILE EMBODIES the end of a history and the possibility of a fu-ture. Living at the end demands consciousness and deliberation. A focus is needed that withstands the confusion and anger, the sense of abandonment, and the feeling that all is lost and empty. Because of this focus, the very end engenders hope beyond the end. The distant embrace is also experienced now.

At that moment the future is not future at all; it is the present in its fullness. The practice of exile is the practice of living in the pres-ent in its fullness and finding in the tension of solitude and solidar-ity glimpses of the future embrace. In some ways we are always at the end of history, even as history continues on. Perhaps the human jour-ney is characterized by the interplay of solitude and solidarity and all attempts to resolve the tension are doomed.

As with God, speculation about the meaning of life in exile is in-evitable. Often meaning is thought to be explored and explained by religion or philosophy. But I find that the meaning of exile and fi-delity is found in the journey itself. Only in the practice of exile does there emerge a clarity. Most of the time, that clarity, achieved for a moment, is gone the next. Moods shift and events alternately bring hope and despair. I find this especially difficult because an assured stability is undermined sometimes without knowing the reason.

There is no system to the practice of exile as there is to the study of theology or philosophy. Perhaps these disciplines attempt to cover over the difficulties of exile. I often hear theologians proclaim the exile as the definitive plan of God. Or they tell us that exile is not exile but rather a plan of redemption. These plans are hidden, to be sure, and esoteric in their formulation. They are understood by the few and the elect. The practice of exile leads away from the definitive and esoteric, the few and the elect. The road is too difficult and uncertain to accept these formulaic answers.

When the exile is long, the questions become even more difficult. The exile is condemned to learn over and over again the limitations of humanity and God. Even the limitations of those who proclaim justice and a journey in exile.

Is there a hope that is honest? A hope that faces the reality of exile as a challenge to overcome the exile? An exilic hope that accompanies the exile even in the darkest time? Perhaps God is that hope. Perhaps hope is what we call God.

Creating a discipline for surviving and navigating the exile is being present to the journey. But being present to the journey of others who are also in exile is important as well. With this dual recognition of our own exile and the exile of others, Jews find our own voice. At least this is how I eventually found my own voice.

This voice I hear is not one of prayer or nonprayer. Or God or no-God. It is a voice less concerned with transmission of the tradition or even definition of what is and what is not Jewish. The division of secular and religious and of Jew and non-Jew ceases to matter in a primary way. I recognize a shared struggle and journey, a similar point of origin and a path that is common.

When I articulate my sense of exile, I experience relief from a lonely and unnamed wandering. Despite the uncertainties ahead, I find naming the exile makes origins and destinations secondary in importance. A common present is accentuated. Even the distance from other exiles is suspended in importance and refocused. I am more certain of my own situation when my voice is heard by others and, as importantly, when it is heard with a new clarity internally among other Jews in exile.

Recognition of myself and others allows the experience of gratitude. Losses incurred in exile can lead to despair. They are confronted by other voices of understanding and by a new self-understanding. A cycle of despair comes with the bleak landscape of exile; it is also interrupted, surprised, intruded upon, and broken. The face of a person opening to the questions that obsess the exile, or the meeting of a person who has been on the path for a longer period of time, startles us. A search that is stalled or is self-referential may be illuminated. A path within a path, a deeper place of journey, may be discovered. What is experienced is less a way out of despair or even out of exile, but another point of entry and reflection. I can be grateful for a fuller expression of life even as that expression also leads to a deeper solitude. This happens to me often: a chance meeting, a phone call telling me the meaning someone else finds in my work. Just when I think the exile is meaningless, something unexpected occurs. I am called out, confirmed, challenged.

A strange gratitude it is that allows the present to interrupt the known and question even the presuppositions of exile itself. For if I already know the path, life closes in on itself. What surprises me also enlightens. The journey I embarked upon continues at a deeper level.

Gratitude is for those who reintroduce vulnerability. In exile, a sense of invincibility and self-righteousness can come into play. What was once criticized in others is internalized until those on the inside and those on the outside become mirror images of one another. If the reason to continue the system for those in power is to remain in power, there can also develop a system of criticism designed to maintain the exile. The exile is here neither to uphold nor overturn a system. Rather, attention is called to injustices that fuel a certain system but also could just as easily fuel another system that takes its place.

Gratitude is part of the practice of exile. If criticism is the origin of exile, gratitude is a guide that enlightens and softens it. To look to the end of exile, as if I enter exile with this goal in mind, is to mistake my life's work for a performance of limited and specified duration.

The task is different, for the practice of exile is open to transformation if history takes a subtle or dramatic turn. Yet even if the turn is dramatic, the practice continues in the new dispensation. Now the practice of exile becomes the practice of embrace, entering the new state of affairs at a depth that limits the possibility of reverting to the previous policies of exclusion and injustice.

Because gratitude is part of the practice of exile, the new reality can be welcomed with the warning that exile may be around the corner. The practice of exile and embrace therefore carry the tension of solitude and solidarity forward in a realism that surpasses the political prognostications of doom and celebration.

I experience this as being simultaneously rooted and open. The practice of exile and embrace frees me to enter into history and different contexts without allowing either participation or withdrawal to predominate. When I am disciplined, I am sober *and* involved, on guard *and* hopeful. Gratitude is balanced by loss. Loss is balanced by gratitude. They inform and enlighten each other. I refuse to be over-whelmed or to succumb.

❧

I OFTEN FEEL that the journey into exile is a preliminary act of confession that takes place long before a people is ready to enact that confession in word and deed. Exile is the beginning of reconciliation and healing for victim and victor. It is the embrace of the suffering and the future on behalf of a community that is silent and betraying its own witness. I think here of Jews and Palestinians who cross the sealed borders as if they do not exist.

Here, as with the question of God, I enter the speculative, as if foretelling can infuse the present with meaning. Yet neither the possibility of God nor the assurance of creating a future is sufficient for the practice of exile to take on depth. In the end, the practice of exile exists within its own frame of reference. I cannot continue on for something beyond my own practice, be it God or a future.

Questions that confront the exile are haunting reminders of the unfinished and unanswerable quality of life's journey. I remain open to gratitude, though it seems so contradictory to the pain of exile. By keeping this possibility before me, I prevent the circle of despair and celebration from closing prematurely.

This is as far as I can proceed. The new diaspora remains a possibility in the making and the Jewish exile—perhaps all exiles in their particularity—can only hope for an inclusion that allows the development of a joint vision and a particular perspective. Vision and purpose emerge from shared and diverse histories. Will the new diaspora eventually welcome Jews in a solidarity that emphasizes diverse practices of exile as gifts to an evolving diaspora? Will Jews one day find their home there? I am torn on this question.

I only have the hope that the practice of exile is requisite to the times in which we live. The questions we cannot answer will remain before us as challenges, confronting complacency and arrogance. Like everyone else, I want assurance of the final destination. Yet if the final destination is assured, exile becomes a strategy awaiting the triumphal procession of victory. The practice of exile would then be as deceptive as those who speak of innocence even as the power they hold conquers and humiliates others. The practice of exile would cease to hold forth the possibility of liberation, a liberation that is always limited.

Can the practice of exile be sustained if liberation is limited? Gratitude is less the fulfillment of dreams than the ability to appreciate commitment as a counterpoint to betrayal. The fruit of exile is that the practice of exile is always ready to reassert itself.

A strange gift to be sure, especially as the surrounding cultures and religions specialize in propositions of fulfillment and certainty. Will the new diaspora one day also demand that such propositions, albeit in its own formulations, be adhered to? I fear that the practice of exile may also develop such orthodoxies. As with the understanding of gratitude, the practice of exile must constantly evolve, refusing to be stuck in its own reflection.

The tensions of solitude and solidarity, secularity and religion, exile and embrace, despair and gratitude, constantly shift. I hold them together as best I can in an eclectic discipline drawn from Jewish history and the new diaspora. The voices that emerge from these tensions are sometimes confusing and they often disorient me. They are, in turn, angry and scandalous. Should I expect something different? *In the practice of exile and the difficult birth of the new diaspora, there is no way home that is not complicity and there is no God at that home but one who assures us of our own righteousness.*

At the very heart of this home and God is a deception seen in the face of the "other" who has been made homeless and lost her sense of God in the catastrophe that we Jews are part of. The home and God suggested beyond complicity and renewal are found in a practice that is lonely and communal, daily and rigorous, and, above all, surprising.

4
Lamentation

IN EXILE the thought of homecoming remains. The tradition surrounding Jewish exile speaks to aspects of the contemporary Jewish condition. I think here of Lamentation 5:20—"Why have you forgotten us completely? Why have you forsaken us these many days?"— and the response of Isaiah 49:15-16—"Even these I may forget yet I will not forget you. See I have inscribed you on the palms of my hands; your walls are continually before me."

The great Christian biblical scholar Walter Brueggemann often quotes these passages and sees God's characteristics of steadfast love and covenant as "more than enough to override the flood, to overcome the absence and shame, and to overmatch the terror of exile." The terror of exile is overcome by the very announcement of God's power to restore a new creation of fidelity and justice. If returning to a home that no longer exists is impossible, the cadences of home are announced. They are practiced in the language of faith, which the exiles have previously embraced.

Brueggemann's sense is that the language of lamentation and complaint so present in the Hebrew scriptures redescribes and reorients the vision and power of those who suffer oppression. It also points to a renewal beyond the present imperial context. Against other gods and powers, exiles then and now "must reflect upon the power of promise, upon the capacity of God to work a newness against all circumstance."

Brueggemann believes that the metaphor of exile is important for contemporary Christians in the West because the social, political, and cultural world they were raised in is being lost. With that loss the patterns of meaning and faith are mocked and trivialized. They are also used as legitimizers of unjust social orders. This very inversion—the gutting of the meaning of Christianity in a culture that holds up Christianity as the normative religion—signals an exilic condition for Christians who want to be faithful to values and a God beyond consumerism and exploitation.

A renewed emphasis on patterns of meaning and response found in the Hebrew scriptures is proposed. Brueggemann thinks the renewal of the preaching and practice of the gospel can only be found through reimaging part of the Christian inheritance. This helps Christians develop critical judgment on society and a language independent of contemporary power. An emphasis on the Jewish response to exile in the Hebrew scriptures functions in the same way for Christians as it did for Jews of ancient times: "Exile did not lead Jews in the Old Testament to abandon faith or to settle for abdicating despair, nor to retreat to privatistic religion." On the contrary, the experience of exile led them to the "most daring theological articulation . . . evoking the most brilliant literature. . . ." Both are grounded in a "sureness of *news* about God that circumstance cannot undermine or negate."

Brueggemann longs for a renewal of Christian faith lived out in the world and shares with aspects of Jewish renewal the idea that dissent and faith are linked. The recovery of God is found in a practice where returning to the sources of tradition helps envision a future beyond the exilic present. Clearly this understanding links aspects of the Jewish and Christian renewal movements.

A connection is found among Jewish and Christian exilic communities that may be important in the formation of the new diaspora. Might what was once joined, then severed almost two thousand years ago, be brought back together? This possibility is important in a renewed and alternative Jewish and Christian discussion, especially against those Jews and Christians who see both religions as affirming power and the state.

Brueggemann's understanding of exile is found within an affluent and at least nominally Christian culture. His exhortation for a new preaching is to those who feel less and less at home in modern culture. These congregants feel uneasy but continue to enjoy the benefits of affluence. Like Jewish renewal, Christian renewal takes place as a critique of the very injustice that most will never relinquish.

Such a renewal carries a status of its own within a renewed church or even among many in a predominantly Christian society that seek meaningful patterns of worship and insight. This status, however, rarely reverses injustice or even challenges it, except in a rhetorical and liturgical way. Renewal and injustice can exist side by side among Christians as it does among Jews.

Brueggemann's many books cover virtually every theme of the Hebrew scriptures and almost always treat each theme in relation to contemporary history and society. Brueggemann clearly avoids any hint of traditional anti-Jewish rhetoric or the sense that the Hebrew scriptures are there solely for Christians to interpret as they will. Yet I find it amazing that he rarely discusses contemporary Jewish life or alludes to the crisis that has generated the Jewish exilic community of our day.

His profound discussion of Christian renewal lacks Jewish content and the attempt to bridge these communities in the present. Though Brueggemann might shy away from such a project because of his sensitivity to the history of Christians trying to define Jews, it is remarkable that he misses this opportunity to form a joint front in the battle to regain a prophetic vision in our time.

I wonder if this inexplicable lack represents a fear that if the crisis of contemporary Jewish life is taken seriously then the future of Christian life will be found within a similar framework. He may fear *the end of Christian history as we have known and inherited it.* Both religions are connected in their origins. Perhaps they are connected in their end as well.

That is why Brueggemann's sense of alternative speech and ritual for Christians who see themselves in exile may represent a safe haven for celebrating renewal while injustice continues. Separation from injustice in word and ritual can be a comfortable way of holding on to a worldview that is assaulted by the powerful who also consider themselves Christian. Like the internal struggle with what it means to be Jewish, the internal struggle with what it means to be Christian can stave off another more devastating assault—the inability of language and ritual to save Christianity and Judaism even in their most beautiful and articulate formulation.

Contemporary Jewish experience is dangerous to Brueggemann's exilic Christians. This is because, while the overt assaults of Western Christianity are seemingly in the past and Christians now have to deal with a nominal Christian culture that does evil in the name of Christianity, a fully articulate and widely celebrated Judaism is violent in its contemporary expression and action. Jewish theologians who have become significant voices in the renewal of Christianity by calling Christians to account for historic anti-Semitism and the Holocaust, thus advising Christians that they must break theologically and politically with injustice in the present, are themselves complicit in injustice. Here I think of the Palestinian people and other peoples with regard to American domestic and foreign policy. As interesting and important as they are in articulating the pain of the Holocaust and the possibility of a just world, the two major Jewish figures in contemporary Christian renewal, Abraham Joshua Heschel and Elie Wiesel, both fail with regard to the Palestinian people.

Do the accusing images facing these figures frighten Christian exiles today because the theologies they produced are compromised by the suffering of the Palestinian people? Along with many other Christians, Brueggemann shies away from these implications precisely, I think, because Judaism and Christianity *are* joined in the larger religious enterprise of the West. "The great problem for exiles is cultural assimilation. The primary threat to those ancient Jews was that members of the community would decide that Jewishness was too demanding or too costly, and simply accept Babylonian definitions and modes of reality," Brueggemann writes. "And surely Jews in exile worried that their young would see no point in the hassle of being Jewish. So it has been with Jews in all their long history of displacement—which is what makes the state of Israel so poignant—the only place where a Jew is not in a hostile, dissonant environment." Is Brueggemann unaware that the question of assimilation has shifted for Jews and that Israel itself is, for many Jews, a profoundly dissonant place to live?

I worry less about Jewish identity per se and more about what Judaism and Jewish life has become. This is true for Christians as well, for Christianity and Christian life have been a problematic from which the crisis of the West issues. The question for Jews and Christians is more than a homecoming in biblical language and themes. Rather, it is the future at the end of Jewish and Christian life. If there is no future for Judaism, can there be a future for Christianity?

The practice of exile for Jews and Christians sacrifices the comfort of reimaging the biblical story in contemporary times. It refuses to use this language to create a future for either tradition. This imagery and language seek renewal, and that renewal can only be built within the framework of injustice. Renewal is an argument for the center of the tradition. It actually strengthens that which it argues against or becomes a competition for who will occupy and direct the next religious establishment. Thus, the appeal to a set of images that are held in common and interpreted differently.

The hope of those in renewal movements is that their interpretation will become *the* normative interpretation. What is called for is patience and working within the communities that share these images. I ask about those who suffer while the long and complex process of renewal takes shape. Are those who suffer relegated to a peripheral status even as they are used as engines for renewal?

᭞

FROM CHRISTIANS, I often hear about the beauty and sacrifice of exilic prophets like Jeremiah and Ezekiel. Though they are cited and explored in depth by many Christians today, the message of Jeremiah and Ezekiel is often harsh. In their view, Jews in exile celebrate a renewed faithfulness within and after the destruction of Jerusalem. Few contemporary Jewish exiles believe that such a renewal will come when Jews finally recognize that their sins lead to punishment, or that only through a faithfulness judged by God and his prophets may Jews flourish in Jerusalem.

The very themes of exile and restoration, banishment and return, captivity and freedom, judgment and faith, captivate Christians who think through their experience in America. Those who actually live through these dichotomies experience a cycle of dislocation, militarism, and marginalization. Their only hope is to end the cycle. To propose that the cycle itself is sanctioned by God—where the faithful one day are the unfaithful the next and the inhabitants of Jerusalem according to the promise are the same Jerusalemites who are exiled because of the violation of the promise—is to sanction violence in the name of God.

I think of Jeremiah's prophecy regarding the destruction of Jerusalem: "Thus says the Lord: Behold, I am giving this city into the hand of the king of Babylon, and he shall burn it with fire. You shall not escape from his hand, but shall surely be captured and delivered into his hand; you shall see the king of Babylon eye to eye and speak with him face to face: and you shall go to Babylon" (Jer. 34:2-3). Ezekiel's pronouncements are even more graphic: "Thus says the Lord God: This is Jerusalem. . . . A third part of you shall die of pestilence and be consumed with famine in the midst of you; a third part of you shall fall by the sword round about you; and a third part I will scatter to all the winds and will unsheathe the sword after them" (Ezek. 5:5, 12).

Ezekiel is speaking to exilic Jews in Babylon about Jews who have remained in Jerusalem. He introduces a further dimension to Jeremiah's own prophecy of an internal split between Jews within and outside of the land. Though they are themselves in exile because of a previous judgment against them, Jews in Babylon are horrified by Ezekiel's vision of what is happening in Jerusalem. Contemporary defilement of God points to their possible return to a purified Jerusalem.

The spirituality that emerges from this cycle is haunting in its beauty. Ezekiel speaks of a divine promise: "A new heart I will give you, and a new spirit I will put within you; and I will take out of your flesh, the heart of stone and give you a heart of flesh. . . . You shall dwell in the land that I gave to your fathers; and you shall be my people, and I will be your God" (Ezek. 36:26-28). Who can forget the haunting lamentation of the psalmist: "By the rivers of Babylon, there we sat down and wept, as we thought of Zion. On the willows there, we hung up our lyres. For there our captors required of us songs, and our tormentors, mirth, saying, 'Sing us one of the songs of Zion.' How shall we sing the Lord's song in a foreign land?" (Psalm 137:1-6).

Yet it remains that this spirituality augurs a return that replaces the indigenous people of the land, Jews and others, who have violated the ordinances of God or who are outside those promises. Few Jewish exiles today embrace a spirituality that sees the expulsion of Jews deemed unfaithful and Palestinians defined as strangers from Jerusalem. Contemporary Jewish exiles cannot affirm the righteousness of their cause over and against the wickedness of contemporary Jewish Jerusalemites and seek their exile as a counterpoint to our own.

The question of punishment and retribution initiated by God or by communities further distances the contemporary exile from the biblical stories and imagery. The generation of theologians reflecting on the Holocaust in the 1960s and 1970s rejected the rabbinic theodicy of explaining Jewish suffering through unfaithfulness to Jewish teaching and therefore to God. If some Jews turned away from traditional forms of Jewish life, this can hardly justify the death of millions of people. One cannot rightly understand the Holocaust as God's call to return to traditional Jewish law and practice. If God does use this suffering as a call to return, what kind of God is this? Can Jews continue to worship such a God? Can I affirm this God?

These questions force a reckoning as we reflect on the Holocaust. Three choices are set before Jews: accept the traditional formula and thus understand the Holocaust as a divine chastisement; reject the suffering of the innocent as connected with Jewish observance and God; reject a God who demands this kind of sacrifice. The challenge before Holocaust theologians is also three-fold: accept the covenant as interpreted traditionally by Jeremiah and Ezekiel, and later by the rabbis, for example; reinterpret the covenant by emphasizing the innocence of Jewish suffering, thereby changing the relationship between the Jewish people and God; reject the covenant altogether as absent or too violent to accept.

Along with the themes of exile and return, the discussion of the covenant is retained in Holocaust theology, though with different understandings and expressions. Instead of the waters of Babylon, the image of the fires of Auschwitz illustrate the exile; the image of return remains Jerusalem, but now as capital of a modern nation. Neither Auschwitz nor Jerusalem are defined by God, except perhaps by God's absence. Exile and return are human—indeed Jewish—responses to a catastrophe that God is powerless to stop.

Though the themes are traditional and distinctly Jewish, power passes from God to the Jewish community. A tradition in contemporary form without God is practiced by the founders of Israel. The other side of exile and return, the possibility of another exile because of unfaithfulness, is excluded. Here the prophetic voices of Jeremiah and Ezekiel are heard only in their words of return. The power of Israel ensures that exile will never occur again.

Also excluded is the positive consciousness of the stranger in the land, a secondary but important theme in the Hebrew scriptures. Carrying through traditional themes in the return to the land, but without the religiosity that also counsels faithfulness and the possibility of punishment if infidelity returns, Jews in Israel are able to do with Palestinians whatever they want. Though the biblical warrants for treatment of the stranger are ambivalent in the Hebrew scriptures and in the history of the Jewish people, a possible brake on the expulsion and denigration of Palestinians is lost.

Since the victory of Israel in the 1967 Arab-Israeli War and the occupation of areas in Jerusalem and the West Bank more connected with Jewish history, an overt Orthodox religiosity is emphasized to legitimate the occupation and argue against it. The designation of stranger comes to the fore again. Within the cycle of exile and restoration the stranger is crucial because the indigenous population looms large in such a scenario. When we are in exile, the stranger occupies the land. After we return the stranger remains. What are we to do with the stranger?

Some Jews enunciate the more positive sense of protecting the stranger. They understand the return to Israel as part of God's will and also feel a responsibility for ethical behavior in that return. The definition of those who live in the land as "stranger," however, already sets them apart as peripheral to the more important enterprise of Jewish homecoming.

The ethical brake within the religious schema has been jettisoned after the Holocaust in the formation of Israel. Therefore that brake can be used against Palestinians to mandate their expulsion on religious grounds, or retained to preserve a peripheral place for Palestinians who are outside the chosen community but nonetheless must be treated as human beings. In both cases, a central question is avoided. This avoidance strikes me as incredible: Can Palestinians in Palestine really be seen as strangers in a secular or religious sense without demeaning their reality and humanity? Can the contemporary practice of exile see European Jews who have emigrated to Palestine and Israel in the context of homecoming while it sees Palestinians who have lived in Palestine and Israel as strangers?

The choice involves another similarity to the earlier exilic period. Exile shattered the cosmic understanding of the Israelites. The theological category of possession of the land under the Davidic dynasty, which was centered in Jerusalem, could no longer be maintained. The people, and especially their leaders, were confronted with a theological and political crisis. They either had to construct an understanding of the world and God in order to transform exile into a new sense of home or reconstruct the world and God in order to explain the exile as a punishment for infidelity. When they emphasized punishment for infidelity, they laid the groundwork for a restoration to the land and to Jerusalem. The choice was between assimilating into Babylonian culture and over time transforming the exile into home, or remaining separate within Babylonia and waiting to return to the promised land.

Though Jewish memory recalls the decision to return as a communal one, the historical reality is quite different. As in every epoch, Jews made diverse decisions. Some affiliated with certain understandings of Jewish life and assimilated to a foreign culture in order to make it their own. Some returned to older, indigenous cults without a belief in Yahweh. Still others retained a belief in Yahweh while embracing Canaanite and Babylonian elements. A small minority adopted Babylonian understandings of the cosmos. In Jeremiah and Ezekiel, these latter patterns of belief and religious practice are condemned. A similar condemnation is found in the Deuteronomic and Holiness materials written by the priests.

Both the prophets and the priests attempt to implement a restoration theology that rescues the promises of Yahweh from a historical crisis of immense proportions. The restoration, however, involves internal and external repression. The restoration of one is the dispossession of the other. In the dispossession of the other, a new exile is created that ultimately speaks to the restored community itself. The rescue of God from a crisis that delegitimates God is itself a crisis, for the God who has been delegitimated must be strengthened to confront the earlier weakness. A restored community carries a God who, though weakened at times, triumphs in the end. In this scenario, a God of inclusion and mutuality is hard to envision; rather the patriarchal God of might and power is much more likely. The cycle of violence also involves God. Times of renewal and restoration are often the most dangerous for coming into contact with a people on a mission from God.

Is this why the celebration of the contemporary Jewish return to the land and to Israel is at the same time a disaster for the Palestinian people? Is this the reason that most Jews in exile from an empowered Jewish community do not relate to biblical language or even the concept of God? Is there a way out of this cycle, a path beyond the themes of exile and restoration?

It is important that contemporary Jewish exiles reject the attempt of Holocaust theologians to employ these traditional themes, albeit in different language. I reject theologies of exile and restoration in any language and seek the end of the cycle engendered in these theologies. I also caution Christians who use the imagery of exile and restoration. There is no way back for Jews or Christians to the biblical images of exile and return. Whatever their initial truths, the cycle of atrocity infuses these images with a darkness that cannot be escaped.

ﯼ

BRUEGGEMANN IS CORRECT that the twin dangers of exile are despair and assimilation, but is wrong about seeing the avoidance of this danger in hope for restoration and separation. How, then, does the exile and the new diaspora proceed? Who do we encounter on this journey? What elements guide us in the practice of exile? Is there a way that I can experience solitude and solidarity and share and communicate it so that it moves beyond the private sphere? If the aim is neither conversion of those around the exile nor perpetual exile itself, is there a purpose of exile beyond fidelity?

Writing of the experience of patients who encountered and found meaning in suffering, Holocaust survivor and psychotherapist Viktor Frankl said that when he could see a meaning in his suffering, there was still suffering, but no longer despair. *"Because despair is suffering without meaning."* Perhaps the same can be said about exile, that when the exiles discover meaning in exile the suffering remains but despair is minimized. Or rather, that there is a constant struggle between despair and meaning without either claiming a final victory.

Instead of alternate sensibilities, I find that the cadences of home *and* homelessness are intertwined. They exist in relation and are part of one another. Lamentation is also part of the journey, though its expression is different depending on circumstance and particularity. Lamentation is despair mingled with hope. It cries out for the end of suffering. This presupposes a purpose in lamentation, a testimony to the possibility of a world where lamentation is minimized and celebration emphasized. Like exile, lamentation is a search for meaning in the context of despair; it attempts to keep both from being disconnected and existing in isolation. Meaning and despair cannot be separate for any length of time without both becoming abstract. Superficiality becomes the norm. The swing is extreme. It breaks the person into pieces.

Frankl referred to this struggle between despair and meaning as coming within the realm of the unconscious God. He defined this God as a transcendent element in humanity that is within us and points toward meaning. Though his work on psychotherapy began before World War II, Frankl's experience in Auschwitz and Buchenwald confirmed his sense that the search for meaning defines the essence of the human. This search is grounded in an unconscious drive toward transcendence that envisions a future beyond the difficulties of the present.

The will to create a future different from the present is a constituent part of the human being. When that is repressed or destroyed, the will to live atrophies. It is this unconscious God, often unnamed or named in different ways by different cultures and traditions, that preserves the integrity of the person, even under degrading circumstances. More than simply the will to live, Frankl believes that the will to moral integrity and witness is at stake. Even death can have a dignity that the circumstances of one's death, especially in the death camps of Nazi Germany, seems to contradict.

Though distant in time and severity, the question of meaning also relates to the understanding of the contemporary exile. If the deaths of millions in the European Holocaust have no meaning, what meaning can a principled exile have?

The traditional definition of martyrdom is at stake in the death of millions of Jews. The larger questions of meaning, commitment, and fidelity are at issue as well. The cycle of destruction is also raised here as one's stance on the meaning of the Holocaust will help determine the roles of witness and power in the present. If the dead of the Holocaust are a testimony to meaninglessness and weakness, then only the will to power can protect and sustain. If the dead of the Holocaust are looked at within the framework of meaning and the desire to end violence, then a different path opens.

The death of millions of Jews is tied to the Jewish exile of our time. The most obvious connection is the one between the Holocaust and Israel. The misuse of the Holocaust as a shield against critical thought and as an assertion of power comes readily to mind. Part of the reason for exile is found here. The search for meaning in exile is also tied to the Holocaust without reference to developments after the event itself. For how we see the dead of the Holocaust, indeed of all peoples who die prematurely in atrocity, is central to the meaning of exile. If the deaths of victims of atrocity are rendered as deaths without meaning, then why embrace a way of life in memory of those dead and those who are dislocated and dying in our time? *If I cannot find meaning in the death of innocents, can I discover meaning in the life of commitment?*

Here memory is crucial. Those who died in the Holocaust cannot be framed in the concepts of meaningfulness or meaninglessness retrospectively. One cannot appeal to the ancient Jewish covenant in its continuance or rejection. Nor can an analysis that posits meaning or chaos in the lives and deaths of the victims be of much assistance.

Much of the lives of the victims is unknown. Their thoughts in life and death are lost to history. We are left with a variety of testimonies that lead in many different directions. What we know is that testimonies and commentary about the Holocaust experience develop a language to communicate a horror that defies language and conceptualization. That which defies conceptualization is conceptualized and a language and order are created in a narrative form that the person writing and speaking and the person reading and listening can understand. One sees this in the work of Lawrence Langer, who seeks to distance the Holocaust from the realm of moral choice. How can there be moral choice in a Nazi universe that closes off such choice? Langer's question is important precisely because it raises the stakes of committing oneself and society to building a world where moral choice makes sense. His refusal to allow any meaning to be laid upon an experience that defies meaning raises the very question of meaning.

I remember the first time I placed these two assertions in motion. I found that Frankl's will to meaning and Langer's denial of meaning have similarities that define their approach almost as much as their more obvious differences. Neither appeals to tradition as salvific or even as capable of responding to the crisis of the Holocaust. Both regard the testimony of the victims as the starting point of envisioning the world. Neither claims that the search for meaning or the inability to continue that search in a meaningless universe can eliminate the pain or lead to a transcendence of the past. There is no restoration of the shattered universe. If religious images, language, and symbols remain, they are interspersed with the reality of death.

For the victims of the Holocaust, the universe must be reconstructed if only to order the story they have to tell. Whatever is helpful is used and whatever is irrelevant is shed. Those who survived the Holocaust are exiles in the most fundamental and horrible way. They are thrown from the known world and thrust into an antihuman reality. They are forever estranged from those who did not experience this horror. The exile of those in the Holocaust is bound up with an experience of horror that is carried to the grave or through a life of survival. This exile cannot be entered by those outside that experience.

I am aware that most of the perpetrators are unrepentant. In an intact universe the guilt of such people should elicit moral sanctions against them. If they commit such acts, they should experience remorse after the fact. The trials of war criminals and the investigative work of scholars point to the opposite. Whether it was Adolf Eichmann or Klaus Barbie or the "ordinary men" who entered into an environment of mass death, their consciences seem extraordinarily clear.

Surely the other side of the question of a meaningful death for victims of atrocity is the punishment of those who perpetrated such acts. But since so few are caught and punished while they are alive, and since in their lives after the massacre they seem to function in normal ways, can I assume a punishment outside of their lives and consciences? Can I assert a religious meaning to the death of millions even if the assassins live on as if nothing happened?

Memory here seems one-sided. The memory of those who died is always on the verge of being lost. Or, as in the monuments built to the victims of the Holocaust, it is on the verge of being politicized and mobilized for the advancement of the living and the destruction of others. In the remembrance of one group of victims, often another oppressed group is created *and* forgotten, as if some people are more important to humanity, to the destiny of the world, and, by inference if not boldly stated, to God. But memory also functions to restore the meaning of lost lives, especially when an obvious meaning is unavailable. For those who survive, memorials function as a search for meaning in a universe that has been violated and shattered.

In the United States Holocaust Memorial Museum in Washington, D.C., Frankl's and Langer's visions are joined, as if both can be asserted, indeed they must be asserted, at the same time. But I also see another cycle continuing in the search for meaning after the Holocaust in the absence of the victims that the memorial also unintentionally signifies. The displacement of the Palestinians is invisible in this "larger" and more "significant" drama. Just as the meaning of the Holocaust is argued about and ordered in architecture and narrative, another challenge to meaning—the dislocation and destruction of Palestine—is obscured.

At least in memorialization, restoration of meaning involves the reassertion of a particular universe and narrative structure that has been challenged and destroyed in a catastrophic event. It is almost as if the individual and the community have difficulty letting go of a world that has been decimated. The recreation of that world is manufactured by those who cannot return to that world and is experienced by those who were never part of that world.

A memorial also seeks to halt time, to deflect our attention of that which comes after: *the catastrophe that is ongoing.* Or the message of the memorial is universalized, obscuring the recognition of particular offenses committed by a grieving people.

5

Memory and the Exile of God

MEMORIALIZATION OF THE VICTIMS of the Holocaust tends to elicit two responses at once. The first is a continuation of the particularity from which the victims came. The second is a universalization that neglects the victims of the mobilization of the memory of the Holocaust. The warning of the first is the protection of memory from usurpation by others. The warning of the second is the projection of memory as an assertion of power and a bulwark against accountability. Too often, Holocaust memorials and museums function as warnings against applying the lessons of the Holocaust to the activities of Jews in the present.

The fear of the memorializing community is the same as the fear the exile faces. By applying the lessons of the Holocaust to the empowered Jewish community, Jews and others might see the universal message to end all atrocity as *the* message. To counter this possibility, Holocaust memorialization continuously sanctions *Jewish* memory. Memory is therefore restrained from drawing lessons for succeeding generations. The universalizing aspect of a memory that indicts complicity in all injustice is disciplined and restrained.

The memory of suffering is unstable in its power and application and must constantly be restored to its proper place. An entire cadre of experts, including those in Jewish and Holocaust studies, are employed to do this. Their task is to assert forever the centrality of the Holocaust as an example of Jewish suffering and its claim on the Western psyche and public policy. That Israel has committed crimes that are warned against by these same memorials—injustice, deprivation of human rights, humiliation, segmenting and ghettoizing a people—is silenced by the very power of the Holocaust narrative.

What is unmentioned and unthinkable is that a Jewish exile has developed in the shadow of these memorials. The very idea that there is now an inclusive liturgy of destruction that must be recounted and remembered—of Jews in Europe and Palestinians in Israel—cannot be thought, even as Jewish exiles embody this understanding. Jews in exile today carry these two memories of destruction within them as part of a continuum that cries out for speech and action. It is the most obvious connection and the one intuitively suggested by the memory of the Holocaust.

If memorialization is defined as the essence of what it means to be Jewish, and if the connection between memorialization and the creation of new victims is central to the contemporary Jewish exile, I fear the gaps between Jewish groups can only widen in the years ahead. Over time, and with the extension of state power, the memory of suffering loses its depth and becomes superficial in its liturgical aspects. By embracing the power of the state to memorialize the victims in America and by shielding Israel from the most obvious scrutiny, the memory of those who suffered is increasingly trivialized. I find it strange that I am sometimes accused of trivializing the Holocaust because of my support of the Palestinians. The opposite is the case. *The trivialization of the memory of the Holocaust victims and the marginalization of the Jewish exile are two aspects of the same process.*

I understand and lift up the Jewish exilic position as fidelity to the memory of those who suffered. Part of the struggle is the reversal of the trivialization of their memory. As a result, the practice of exile takes on another dimension. I experience the struggle to be faithful to the present as a way of rescuing the victims of the Holocaust from a memorialization that empties their death of significance. I carry on the discussion of the meaning of the suffering in the Holocaust by doing what was largely neglected in the Holocaust—opposing power that dispossesses and destroys in the name of innocence and redemption.

For me, memory becomes less a debate about humanity or God. The thought of restoration or redemption of memory and significance is left to those who operate within systems of empowerment. In some ways, those outside these systems are less articulate about these questions and without sure definitions of the way forward

within empowerment. Without institutional framework and structure, the lessons of the Holocaust are less formulaic.

My experience is that the organization and projection of memory
of those in power have further deprived those outside that organization of a language of memory. The exile can only embody this memory, carrying it forward as if hurled into an unannounced future. We
flee on a path that is without name or assured destination. The possibility of restoring memory, of returning to that which is known, to
resting comfortably with those who have the "proper" response to the
Holocaust, is impossible.

ﻋﺖ

IN EMBODYING THIS MEMORY, I cross a boundary from which there is
no return. In crossing this boundary, I ask whether the boundary of
the known is the boundary of our destiny. Is memory itself the
boundary that has been crossed? Or has memory propelled me to
seek another destiny?

The memory of suffering is like the memory of God. Carried in
flight, it is part of the tension of solitude and solidarity. The aloneness of one who suffers is found within the exile, too, as part of the
journey, just as a once present and now absent God is part of that
aloneness. It is also part of solidarity because both the memory of
suffering and the memory of God force those who experience this
tension from patterns of injustice even without a known destination.
The memories of suffering and God point less to a return to safety or
belief than a journey beyond both.

Where others rest, secure in memorialization and even in the debate about God, the exile refuses to be secure in either sensibility.
For as another violation occurs and a new memory of suffering is created, the memory of God becomes still more distant. Can the exile do
anything but protest a blindness that replicates what is being
mourned?

The further violation changes the memory. Now another people is
included in the memory of suffering and the memory of God. The
Holocaust can no longer be mourned on its own, despite its historical
singularity, because ultimately the issue is not history in and of itself.
The issue is always the meaning of history as interpreted by those who
come after. The exile is one who comes after the Holocaust *and* Israel.

Solidarity with the Jewish *and* Palestinian people is one solidarity. Militarization deepens the solitude bequeathed by the Holocaust. The wounds of the Holocaust are reopened. Healing becomes more distant.

So, too, with the question of God, like the debate about meaning in suffering. I find the memory of God's presence and the absence of God in the Holocaust an unresolvable problem. Still I find it difficult to see how the next stage of the journey can arise when the memories of suffering and God are used to inflict injury on another people. Militarizing memory and God can only further distance us from the healing and presence that time, confession, and reconciliation may offer. I wonder if in carrying the memory of suffering and God into exile, the exile offers the possibility of healing and reconciliation as a way out of a cycle that promises little but pain.

Solidarity is thus a complex process of reaching out to another people with the simple demands of justice and in so doing reaching within for the possibility of healing. *The crossing of the boundary, the refusal of the boundary that has been drawn as the boundary of our destiny, is the joining of justice and healing. This joining also raises the possibility of a God beyond remembrance, a God who becomes present if the cycle of displacement and degradation ends.*

The memory of suffering and the use of suffering as a blunt instrument of oppression have rendered the language of God mute. That language can become articulate again only as the cycle of pain is reduced and the dynamic of solitude and solidarity is transformed.

As with the memory of suffering and God, the dynamic of solitude and solidarity is contextual, responsive to historical conditions, and open to transformation. The world looks quite different from a perspective of injustice or the perspective of a fight for justice. Solidarity itself elicits new questions and demands new responses. The exilic position, like the memory of suffering and God, is placed in motion.

The search for meaning in the death camps remains. It now includes contemporary suffering. Meaning in suffering cannot be thought through in solitude, in only one place without reference to the suffering of others. A solidarity with the Palestinian people means that the very solitude that Jews experienced can no longer be understood apart from the solitude Palestinians experience at our hands.

The same is true with the question of God. Can the question of God exist today for Jews without reference to Palestinians? Can it be that the presence of God is finally reasserted for Jews as the absence of God becomes clear for a people on the other side of Jewish power?

To move forward is to understand that when redemption is a disaster for the "other," redemption cannot be claimed. Disaster for the other is, at the same time, disaster for the "innocent." The memory of contemporary suffering and ancient religiosity is sullied in the process. Memory becomes distant and abstract. It is a formula that is recited but no longer believed in.

When the dissenters arrive, often belatedly, memory is used against them. It is as if that memory is deemed foreign to the journey of the people. Thus the prophetic word is acknowledged only in its application *to another time and to other circumstances*. The past is used to legitimate certain acts and, in reference to other acts, is turned against itself. Selection of texts and selective applicability to different situations becomes the order of the day.

When used to further the cycle of violence and to quell the voices of dissent, memory is violated even as it is asserted. Ultimately, the memory itself is abandoned by those who embody it. When used to perpetuate the cycle of violence the very memory of suffering renders the prophetic mute. Even as they are carried across boundaries by those thrust into exile, the words of the prophets are difficult to articulate.

Still, muteness is relative. By embodying the biblical and Holocaust narratives in the crossing of boundaries to the other, the boundaries of Jewish destiny are affirmed in a new way. The voice that carries the exile to the "other" is stifled and awaiting a new articulation.

At the end of Jewish history, the memory of suffering, even the memory of God, is ready to begin another chapter of this long history. I wonder who speaks more boldly of these memories: those who memorialize the dead in institutional and liturgical settings or those who recognize and accompany the victims created in the shadow of the Holocaust.

ىۏ

RECENTLY, Rachel's Tomb was renovated and expanded. Located on the outskirts of Bethlehem right across from an Israeli checkpoint, Jewish worshipers were exposed to disturbances caused by Palestinian youth who were protesting the policies of closure and continued occupation under the Oslo process.

To protect these worshipers, an extensive renovation of the tomb area was completed. The walling-in of the compound and other measures secured the compound from Palestinians who live in the area. The ceremonial opening of the tomb found the Israeli defense minister, Yitzhak Mordecai, speaking of the Jewish return to Israel "after 2,000 years of longing." During the ceremony, Israeli soldiers surrounded the tomb and stood on the rooftops adjacent to it.

When I visit Israel I often pass this shrine on my way to Bethlehem. Bethlehem is part of Palestinian territory and to visit Palestinian friends, I need to cross the checkpoint there. The contrast between a religious shrine on the one hand and a military checkpoint on the other is startling. I see religious Jews guarded by soldiers strolling in and out of the shrine. I also see hundreds of Palestinians making their way through the checkpoint where they are identified and searched. They wait for hours to pass through. Sometimes they are turned away without reason or cause. The sense of violated dignity is in the air. Jews move freely in and out of the shrine. Under the watchful eyes of the Israeli soldiers, the prayers continue. Often the praying Jews have automatic weapons slung over their shoulders.

The image one is left with is instructive. The boundaries of contemporary Jewish life are framed by memorialization of the dead, and the religious obligations in the land are protected by Jewish soldiers. Both are surrounded by a hostile indigenous population. With the sealing of the borders, the soldiers guarding the worshipers are permanent. They are now part of the landscape.

Will the Jewish return always carry this image even under the guise of peace? Is the occupation of most of Palestine essentially permanent, even if some areas are declared Palestinian? Do these soldiers guard me? Do they also guard God?

Guarding me. Guarding us. Guarding God. These images are haunting. They are also revealing. The connection to the state can, at least in the United States, be accomplished without a show of arms. The arms are there, of course, but neatly tucked away or carried by others in a foreign policy rhetoric that is not distinctly Jewish. The Israeli soldiers are carrying out policies that are made by Jews and, like in America, articulated with a language of innocence and redemption.

The confluence of the American and Jewish rhetoric, which suggests that both nations are joined in a moral crusade to which others object at their physical and moral peril, cannot continue indefinitely. Moreover, as time goes on the links between the American-Jewish and Jewish-Israeli communities and the rhetoric that has joined the United States and Israel are bound to fray. For though both communities and nations have been in relative harmony for many years, the experience of Jews in America and Israel is very different. Some have speculated that two different cultures are being created. In the end they will be linked only by the past and a common naming as Jews. I find it difficult to disagree with this analysis.

The ongoing dispute about the question of who is a Jew subsumes Jewish energies and angers Jews far more than the question of Jewishness raised by the treatment of Palestinians. In some ways, the "who is a Jew?" dispute in overt religious matters has buried the deeper challenge to Jewishness raised by the need for soldiers to guard the "return" of Jews to the land.

The call for Jewish unity is heard throughout Jewish communities in America. Is that unity already diminished to a fine point of rhetoric? What does unity mean if the substance of Jewish life is gutted? Is the end of Jewish history at hand? Is the other side of Rachel's Tomb, the massacre at Hebron, carried out by Baruch Goldstein, a physician and religious Jew who saw it as his religious duty to massacre Muslim worshipers at the tombs of Abraham and Sara?

So, too, the assassination of Yitzhak Rabin is mourned and commemorated. In his death he has become almost a saint. In life, Rabin was assuredly more complicated. After all, he was one of the founders of Israel who, among other actions, supervised the "cleansing" of Palestinians from parts of the land. He is the one who ordered the physical crushing of the first Palestinian uprising. It was his policy of might and beatings that horrified Palestinians—and Jews as well.

And there is more. Though he reluctantly shook the hand of Yassir Arafat on the White House lawn in 1993, the Oslo agreements

Rabin signed help continue the cycle of victory and defeat. Though the overall recognition is symbolically important, the details of Oslo remain a victory for Israel over a defeated Palestinian people. Though these agreements are widely heralded as a significant breakthrough, the opposite lesson can be drawn: they show how much Jews have learned to tolerate injustice as a way of peace.

Even with this caveat the anger among some Jews toward Rabin was palpable. The celebration and denigration of Oslo and the assassination, coming soon after the massacre in Hebron, demonstrate the narrowing of Jewish concern and attention.

Has Jewish life narrowed to the images of an agreement such as Oslo, the atrocity in Hebron, the assassination of Rabin, and the militarization of a tomb that symbolizes the birth of the Jewish people? Does this narrowing portend a future for the Jewish people? And do those who guard the return, the soldiers, to be sure, but also Jewish leadership in America and Israel, guard me as well?

Guarding the return is seen as guarding Jewish history. In guarding Jewish history, there is the implicit assumption of guarding the Jewish covenant. In guarding the Jewish covenant, the Jewish God is protected. So the logic proceeds. Within this syllogism is the anxiety that to guard Jewish history, the covenant, and God is to guard concepts and events that are unstable, disputed, difficult to define, dissolving, or absent.

Can this guarding occur without undermining the foundation of these concepts and ultimately raising doubts about their efficacy and existence? Or do these doubts themselves necessitate a guard to solidify and make visible what is elusive and invisible? Guarding the return is one way of crying out that never again will doubts be voiced, this even as doubts increase dramatically. As the void increases, so does militarization. Normalization becomes a rhetoric to justify and legitimate this situation as if there is no way beyond the cycle of void and violence.

Hence the militarization of Jewish rhetoric and actions are coupled with a secular and religious piety that denies the possibility of such militarization. When Jews are confronted with this militarization, it is treated as an impossibility because such a cycle, at least in the Jewish imagination, is frozen. The memorialization of the dead and the image of innocent Israeli soldiers freeze Jewish history in a past that is receding.

ورت

FOR ME THE QUESTION REMAINS: Can the covenant be guarded? Can the covenant be embraced by capturing, defining, and instrumentalizing it? I wonder also if the covenant can be embraced through an inclusiveness that costs little—a liturgical renewal for example—while the centrality of justice is ignored. When Israel, however, defines the boundaries of Jewish life and some Jews refuse those boundaries but are powerless, what are we to do? Simply rail against those who guard the covenant and claim it for themselves, as if the covenant was not given to all Jews at Sinai and is therefore binding for all Jews today?

A fractured covenant claimed by competing perspectives is something other than the Jewish covenant. As has happened previously in Jewish history, it may be the context for a new understanding of the covenant and covenantal responsibility. Yet as history testifies, those who subvert the meaning of the covenant today often guard it tomorrow.

Those who compete to define the covenant guard their own definition within the contemporary struggle. Like the former guardians, they seek to set the limits of dissent and the parameters of thought. The military guards at Rachel's Tomb are similar to those intellectuals who guard the pages of *Commentary,* the once progressive and now conservative Jewish magazine, and *Tikkun,* the progressive Jewish magazine of today. I wonder if the progressives in power would be so different in the claims of their orthodoxy from the ones they seek to supplant.

I approach again the dynamic of renewal within a tradition and whether the prophetic call is part of a cycle of renewal and retrenchment. Is this part of the cycle of exile and return found in the scriptures? Regardless of the reinterpretation of meaning and perspective, those who claim orthodoxy or who seek to supplant orthodoxy with a new vision—those who compete for the center of the tradition—accept a framework that is already in existence. The prophet as an agent of renewal believes in the same unfolding and destiny as those whom he seeks to topple. Claiming this destiny for the new era of Jewish life, can he help but replicate the same practices that afflict all orthodoxy—territoriality, militarism, and thought control—and the feeling that Jews who do not abide their parameters are lost to

the Jewish community? Perhaps this is why the leaders of Jewish renewal in the United States have, through a creative and nonestab-
lishment process, ordained themselves as rabbis.

The stakes are high. The covenant originates at Sinai and creates
a people who seek a community formed around a particular God.
The following generations live within this particular commitment or
stray from it. If there is some kind of ontological connection with this
particular path so that it must be maintained, fought over, suffered
and struggled for, then the new rabbis have the same responsibility as
the old rabbis. Each generation has a sense that its claims are closest
to the origins and to God.

After years spent rejecting binding authority of texts and interpretation, the new rabbis rediscover these same texts and interpretation and find them binding when they interpret them. The
method of discerning Jewish commitment, the covenant, which was
originally dismissed by the new rabbis as a guide to their lives, is
found in their later years to be authoritative as they give voice to it.
The battle lines shift in this rediscovery between the establishment
and the subversives. Each seeks the establishment position.

Is the clash of these forces simply a ploy for power in an ever-
diminishing symbolic and cultural field? Do they represent a fear of
the future where these texts and interpretations, the very idea of
covenant itself, has lost its force? These symbols and texts are important for the individuals who interpret them. I find it difficult to
imagine them commanding assent from the majority of Jews living
today. The future is still another question. The rebellion against the
powerful and the later embrace of those symbols and texts is often
shrugged off by the next generation as irrelevant to its own concerns.

In my own mind there is little to suggest a return to the tradition,
however interpreted, at least for the majority of Jews. The rebellion
against the new establishment will most likely signal the entrance
into a different set of symbols and texts altogether. The new rabbis
will then be in the position of presiding over a victory that is empty
of the young and the majority. It could be that the new rabbis assume
their authoritative positions as the rabbinic office itself passes into
history.

As the worshipers gather at Rachel's Tomb, this battle for the tradition seems almost beside the point. For what does the guard matter when the old and new establishments either perpetuate or are

powerless to stop the force that draws the boundaries of contemporary Jewish existence? After the rebellion, what is there to inherit? What will come together to form the identity of the next generation of Jews? The Holocaust and Israel have formed the nexus for Jewish identity in the latter half of the twentieth century. Both will be more distant in experience and geography for most Jews in the twenty-first century. What, then, will be the content of Jewish identity?

In a strange twist, many Jews in Israel do not identify themselves as Jews but rather as Israelis, prompting one observer to label Israelis "Hebrew-speaking Gentiles." The vocal minority of Orthodox Jews in Israel struggles against these other Israelis and it is likely that the identity emerging from this struggle will focus on the state, articulated in either a secular or a religious way.

At some point a compromise will occur and a viable Israeli civil religion will take root. This civil religion will be part of a separate nation and quite different from the civil religion that many Jews affirm within the United States. For the most part, the two largest Jewish communities in the world are being separated further into those who affirm as primary to their identity a series of symbols that are either foreign to their history, as in the United States, or are assuming meanings beyond what the tradition can carry, as in Israel.

In both nations a general assimilation of Jews and Judaism to the state has already occurred. The energy of Jewish intellectuals and religious leaders is spent bringing that assimilation into conformity with the symbols and texts of Jewish culture and religion. This, as the main thrust of the tradition is compromised almost to the point of disappearing.

The struggle to retain a particularity within the general framework of assimilation to the state will continue. It may even intensify. As the covenant becomes less specific and less important, its guardians increase and cut across the religious and political spectrum. Such is the way when communities become empowered.

In the end, those who argue within empowerment for the retention and expansion of the tradition become guardians of a history that is violated even as it is invoked.

6

Auschwitz at the
End of Jewish History

IN 1992 I TRAVELED TO AUSCHWITZ. I was invited to join a delegation
of Jewish leaders going to the site. The delegation was sponsored by
the Oxford Centre for Post-Graduate Hebrew Studies. It was four
years after my Jerusalem dream. When I received the invitation, I re-
called that dream and its significance in my life. I felt my travel to
Auschwitz was somehow tied to that dream, though I was unsure
how. Would I find a calling to testify here as well?

Our task was to advise officials of the Auschwitz museum in their
quest to more accurately portray what had occurred there during the
Nazi era. The fall of the Soviet Union and the new-found freedom in
Poland precipitated a re-evaluation of the Auschwitz narrative presented to the public.

Before the fall of the Iron Curtain, the narrative at Auschwitz emphasized the evils of fascism and the deaths of over a million people
during its operation as a death camp. The dead were identified in national groupings, leaving Jews to be counted within those nationali-
ties. Left unstated was the fact that Jews were singled out for death
and that the great majority of the dead at Auschwitz were murdered
because they were Jews. We went to Auschwitz to change this narrative and to emphasize the Jewish component of death.

Most of the delegates were university professors and rabbis from
the United States and Europe. There were a few representatives from
Israel. For the most part, they were liberal in religion and politics
and, like much of the Jewish community in the West and Israel, rea-
sonably affluent. We lived in a comfortable present as we visited an
extremely difficult past.

The comfort also hid a conflictual present, as the first Palestinian uprising was in full swing. As I embarked on this trip to Poland, I wondered whether the tension between past and present would be evident and how this might affect the delegates' sense of the future.

Would visiting this place of death be a catalyst for a vision that seeks to own up to the history we were creating and move Jewish life in a different direction? Could solidarity with the dead bring into being a solidarity with a future where there is no more death? Would resources surface that signal solidarity with the dead *and* the living? Would the living be defined exclusively as Jewish or would the dead demand a broader solidarity?

At Auschwitz we set ourselves apart. Our vision was limited. Even though few of us keep kosher at home, the organizers had kosher food flown in from Switzerland. There was little discussion about contemporary Jewish life, especially aspects of our empowerment in America and Israel.

I was also set apart. Some of the delegates knew of my work on behalf of Palestinians. The details of my position were unimportant. Few had read my writing or were interested in doing so. The situation sometimes was comical, as when roommates were assigned to defer the cost of the hotel rooms. No one would volunteer to be my partner. Some delegates refused to speak to me or even make eye contact with me. The hotel was old and the stairway wide. Once when I was walking up the stairs to my room, a colleague who had avoided me was also climbing the stairs to his room. I deliberately slowed down to see if he would engage me. He slowed down to make sure that the engagement did not occur. To see grown men act like this was humorous and depressing.

But I also met others who were unassuming and gracious. One was an Israeli who worked at Yad Vashem, the Holocaust memorial in Israel. His name was Mordecai Atetz and when he greeted me in the hallway on the first night after my arrival, we fell into a rambling and fascinating discussion. His parents were survivors of the Holocaust. Like many survivors they spoke little to their children about their experience. They wanted to protect their children from the horror and themselves from reliving a chapter of their life they wanted closed forever. As he grew older, Mordecai felt a need to recover the history that his parents lived through but were reticent to disclose. He affiliated himself with Yad Vashem so that he could travel through Eastern

Europe and videotape other survivors telling their stories. The hour was late as that generation was reaching its end.

Mordecai was a small player in this affair. He had no academic credentials or at least he did not present any. He simply traveled the back roads looking for anyone who would talk to him of those dark times. He stayed in cheap hotels where restaurants were nonexistent and coffee was hard to secure in the early morning hours. As we talked, he invited me into his room. His suitcase was huge and reflected the way he traveled. As he was unpacking I noticed a panoply of items; an iron, a large container of hot chocolate, a smaller container of coffee, morning sweets, and a small hot pot that boiled water. When I asked where these items came from he answered simply that his mother packed them for these trips. She knew that the journey would be difficult. She wanted him to have at least a few comforts from home.

Mordecai was the human face to our delegation. He was also naive. His search was for survivors and to record their testimony. He was an Israeli to be sure, but without ideology or the desire to own or use the Holocaust. Later during our stay, Mordecai became incensed by some of the posturing of the academics from the United States. His English was passable but halting. He asked to address the delegation in Hebrew and all assured him this was fine. He started quickly to his point but soon the delegates asked him to continue in English. Their credentials as Jewish scholars forced them to assent to Hebrew. Their inability to carry on a conversation of any length in Hebrew halted Mordecai's presentation. Afterward he asked me why he had been asked to change back to English. I told him it was part of the hypocrisy we were all involved in. He thought that as the child of survivors and an Israeli his voice should be heard. The reality was different. Most of the delegates felt they owned Auschwitz. Any vision that differed from theirs was suspect no matter the background or experience that formed that voice.

During our stay, a Jewish Auschwitz survivor group from France arrived by train and commemorated their own suffering by stopping at various places in the camp, reading their reflections, and praying for those who had died. Some delegates viewed this as a "pilgrimage," a Jewish expression of the stations of the cross. When Elie Wiesel's autobiographical work *Night,* a short and moving book about his own time in Auschwitz, was discussed, he, too, was criticized as having assumed a "priestly" status among Jews, a reference to the Catholic institution of priesthood.

Commemoration of Auschwitz was seen as authentic only within a narrow spectrum. I quickly understood that the idea that Palestinians could also be seen within the framework of Auschwitz—if only the possibility that mourning the Jewish dead instructed Jews to refuse dislocating and murdering others—was beyond discussion. Such thoughts were seen as blasphemy to be condemned.

Alternative ways of commemorating the past were frowned upon. What suggestions did the delegation have in this regard? Auschwitz was the end for so many Jews, and yet many Jews live today in changed circumstances. What was suggested for a possible future?

Auschwitz was receding in time. The behavior of Israel was challenging this memory. Many were using the Holocaust to legitimate Israel's violent response to the first Palestinian uprising. Others used the Holocaust to condemn the cycle of violence that Jews were now furthering. I thought that the delegation had a responsibility to articulate a future in relation to the past and the present. Could we pretend that the memory of the Holocaust, abused by the Soviet influence in Poland, was not also being abused by Jews in the present?

Jewish-American and Israeli groups also came to remember the dead. These groups came to Auschwitz to heighten commitment in the present. For Jewish-American youth, the experience of Auschwitz is to make them aware of the perilous times Jews lived in and may live in again some day. The message is that the core of Jewish identity is remembering the Holocaust and identifying with Israel. For Israeli youth, the message of Auschwitz is to remember their sense of Jewishness, why Israel was founded, and the need to build Israel into an even stronger nation. Auschwitz as a memory defines the present. I found it difficult to pretend that our journey was only about the past.

The moment of decision arrived when the museum officials asked us to suggest the appropriate narrative to present to the hundreds of thousands of visitors to Auschwitz each year. Auschwitz could be presented historically as if it had nothing to do with the present. Yet this was clearly untrue. Why else would we be there? Auschwitz could be presented as a memory to interact with the present, as in fact it already and unavoidably did. In what way should that be seen?

Auschwitz could also be seen as a memory that should influence the future. This too had to be part of the mission of this delegation. What future vision could we articulate?

The details of the narrative became important. Such issues as the anti-Semitism of the Nazi time, where Jews were transported from, and what happened to Jews at Auschwitz were all part of our discussions. Even more important was the overall framework of the narrative. What does Auschwitz mean? Here the end of the narrative is of utmost importance if Auschwitz has meaning for the future. Our task was remembering for the future as there could be no memory for itself. What would come at the end of the narrative?

I was somewhat surprised when the most obvious ending, Israel, was dismissed at the outset. As to Holocaust and Israel, each stood on its own. What about Israel with other Jewish communities at the end of World War II, illustrating the rebuilding of Jewish life after mass death? The answer here was also no. The delegation decided that the end of the narrative at Auschwitz is death itself. Auschwitz stands alone in its starkness. What about a world in mourning and rebuilding using Auschwitz as a guide for refusing death and affirming life? The answer remained the same.

Since most of the delegates were invited to Auschwitz precisely because they had spent their professional lives remembering Auschwitz, I felt this refusal dishonest. Underlying their decision was a palpable fear that surfaced toward the end of our journey. Many delegates felt that the Holocaust was being used by too many groups. It was in the process of becoming an ideological tool. Auschwitz should be left in its own integrity.

The decision to mark Auschwitz as off-limits seemed to me another strategy to lay claim to the event. The delegates felt the use of the Holocaust by Jews and others was out of control. Soon the actuality of the suffering might be lost in this use. The feeling that Auschwitz was being "lost" is already demonstrating a stake in "owning" the memory of Auschwitz in a particular way. Lost to whom? Whose claim is being lost?

I wondered whether this sense of loss extended beyond the "pilgrims" and the "high priest" to the contradictory images that the Jewish use of power adds to this memory. Auschwitz as a memory for the future was clearly seen as a danger that had already arrived. Jews and others were trying to build a future out of the ashes of

Auschwitz and that future threatened the delegates' sense of propriety, and piety as well.

Ownership of the Holocaust memory provides a platform for the delegates' sense of contemporary life. Placing the Holocaust clearly in the past is already a statement to that end. Those who use Auschwitz are warned that they are endangering the sanctity of the victims. Uncoupling Auschwitz from contemporary Jewish theology and from Israel is a decision about the use of memory. Were the delegates uncoupling Auschwitz from the future?

Contemporary Jewish identity revolves around the linking of the Holocaust and Israel as the delegates are quite aware; they are prime movers in this enterprise. Hence the impossibility of such a suggestion. Rather, the suggestion provided a way of protecting the connection as it had stood. There could be no expansion beyond the Jewish world and erosion from a posture of innocence to one of culpability.

The public discussion of the Holocaust had proliferated. It could no longer be controlled. Other sufferings had taken place since the Holocaust. The innocence of Israel was now being challenged by some Jews, by Palestinians, and by many in the international arena. The 1980s had brought Israel into a global, often negative limelight. The Israeli invasion of Lebanon and the policy of might and beatings to quell the first Palestinian uprising was international news and provoked international concern. The occupation of the West Bank and Gaza then stretched more than two decades despite its violation of international law. To much of the world the occupation seemed to be taking on the character of annexation.

The delegates were in an almost impossible situation. They could not place Auschwitz in continuity with the Jewish past as if Auschwitz was simply another event of Jewish suffering to be worked through within the ancient covenant. Nor could they place Auschwitz as a break with that continuity. Instead, they saw Auschwitz suspended in time, without direction. As if history had stopped. As if the trains were still being loaded with Jews. As if the camps had just been liberated.

If history is suspended we can mourn Auschwitz. The Jewish world, and we ourselves, retain an innocence. We can hold others accountable to a political and moral standard that cannot be applied to us. A directionless Auschwitz points neither to the past nor the future. An Auschwitz protected from use, at least in the minds of the delegates, is an Auschwitz mobilized to protect Jews in the present. But what content could our delegation bring to this protection?

Those who place Auschwitz in continuity with the Jewish past were ridiculed. This was the fate of the French "pilgrims" and the "high priest" Elie Wiesel. Others, like myself, who suggest that the victims of the Holocaust can only be honored by including those whom we are displacing in the present, were greeted coldly by some and ignored by others. The delegates' proposal was a narrative with death as an end and pleas for site preservation. The physical plant of Auschwitz is to be preserved so that the ashes of the dead are respected and those Jews who come and mourn can do so in dignity.

As I left Auschwitz, I wondered if the place they sought to preserve was itself a place of pilgrimage. It was *their* site, *their* interpretation, *their* journey, and thus carried *their* stamp of authenticity. But for those who come to Auschwitz after us, what do we leave them?

In a guard tower looking over the fields of Auschwitz, a group gathered to say the Jewish prayer for the dead. The mourners' Kaddish has been recited for millennia over the Jewish dead, though death is never mentioned in the prayer itself. The prayer is one of gratitude for life God has given us and for the future where the kingdom of God will come to fruition. It was a dramatic moment as people of different religious and political perspectives came together in tribute to the dead.

After the Kaddish we walked through the decaying camp. What had it been like in this place of death? Reading of Auschwitz and being there are two different things. The ground itself is silent with a poignancy beyond description. What do these prayers mean here where the killing occurred? What can they mean to those who did not experience the killing and were born after this event of mass death?

The discussion about meaning during and after the Holocaust takes on a different dimension at the death site itself. The reality of human life and death, its fragility and preciousness, life in its diversity and contradictions, take hold. The theoretical discussions, as important as they are in certain contexts, move to the background. Those who became victims are also demystified. Before becoming victims of the Nazi atrocity, they existed in life in the most ordinary of ways.

In death the victims of Auschwitz are elevated as if they carry an ontological message. Their reality—a shared humanity, a background of Jewishness, a home in Europe—was something different. Sharing a fate does not homogenize a group except in the eyes of those who mourn their death. Can death bring together that which is disparate?

The Kaddish places the dead into an understandable continuity. In reality those who died in Auschwitz came from many places and perspectives. Is the Kaddish a way of managing diversity and conflict, burying the dead so that the living can take hold?

The Jewish tradition has a place for mourning and for the end of mourning. The Kaddish is the beginning of mourning, as the dead are remembered by praising life. The intense schedule of mourning diminishes over time. The tradition recognizes the need to mourn and the need to continue with life. To refuse to mourn condemns the dead to oblivion; to dwell on death precludes a future. In the Jewish tradition the dead are buried quickly, remembered yearly, so that the movement of life is emphasized.

The discontinuity that death introduces is rarely affirmed in Jewish ritual. The tasks that ensure the continuity of life are emphasized. Neither a person nor a people can live if dwelling in the past. The tradition recognizes that the memory of the dead can overshadow life and become an excuse for not facing life as it is.

As our journey came to an end, one theologian suggested that the rules of mourning in the Jewish tradition should be applied to Auschwitz. Auschwitz, like the body of the individual Jew, should be buried with the Kaddish emphasizing life. At first intense mourning is needed. Then mourning on a yearly basis should take place. Auschwitz as a physical place should be left to decay to the rhythms of nature and the exigencies of history. Auschwitz should become a memory more distant with time. Otherwise the shadow of death will be mistaken for life itself.

There were signs of life at Auschwitz. There was the normal discourse about family and jobs, about old friends, books to be written, sermons to be preached. Auschwitz was a preoccupation but it was also a break from our normal life and the routines associated with it.

We came from and returned to a life so different from the death we mourned at Auschwitz that the distance between past and present is great. I felt an unbridgeable gap between the two because the life we lead today is so radically different from the lives led by those who perished in Auschwitz. The gap can be analyzed theologically and even politically, yet the most obvious gap is life itself. Time moves on whether we mourn Auschwitz as a way of preserving it, or allow it to decay so that Auschwitz relinquishes its central role in Jewish life. The context of contemporary Jewish life is so radically different that theological categories seem almost contrived.

I wonder whether the discussion about meaning at Auschwitz was a discussion about the dead or about the living. I also wonder whether our discussion is relevant to the coming generations. The meaning of life is found in the present. Often that meaning is projected back upon the past as if the past bequeaths what we ourselves discover.

In the historical scheme of things, Auschwitz is one event among many. Death, as horrible as it was, was experienced before Auschwitz and has been afterward. Did Jews in Auschwitz experience death differently from Jews who have been murdered at different times in history? Did Cambodians slaughtered in the killing fields experience less terror and loss than the Jewish victims of the Nazi era? One thinks of the genocide in Rwanda and the mass killings in Bosnia and Algeria as the twentieth century came to a close. Does the difference in numbers, context, geography and ethnic identification, change the experience and meaning of death?

Meaning is struggled for in every generation and in every context. In this struggle Jews are hardly distinct. The recognition of a common struggle for meaning within various experiences of atrocity hardly minimizes Jewish suffering. Does the desire to own the Holocaust mean that we fear letting go of Jewish suffering? Do we fear that the Jewish claims to uniqueness will be lost if the uniqueness of the Holocaust is challenged?

Perhaps the delegates understood that Jewish history has changed because of Auschwitz *and* because of what Jews have done to Palestinians. After all, we were meeting at a time when Israeli jails were full of Palestinian resistors. Hospitals were full of Palestinian children who were paralyzed for life or dying. Perhaps the delegation realized that it lacked the imagination to project a Judaism that survives both being a victim and being an oppressor.

ఆక్ష

IN THE MIDST of the delegation was Gillian Rose, a Jewish-British philosopher. In her mid-forties, she had risen in the ranks of European philosophy. In doing so, she returned to aspects of Jewish law and tradition. As her worked evolved, she brought the two schools of thought and practice into dialogue.

What struck me about Gillian, however, was less her philosophy than her vision and commitments. Unlike many of the male Jewish leaders, she reached out to the Polish people we met as historical victims of Nazism and Soviet communism. She was also aware of the difficulties that the Poles experienced with the end of communism. Gillian was saddened by the delegation's lack of focus on the people who hosted us. I was also struck by her comments about a God who was present among us—so close, she said, that we were unable to perceive it—and by her care for her first teacher of philosophy who was dying of AIDS. We spent time together during that week and became friends.

Gillian's philosophy is best summed up with the term she developed, "broken middle." The broken middle is a philosophical position that allows the past to speak to the realities of the present without determining it. Conversely, the present is indebted to and needs the past. If either the past or the present is seen as independent, a superficial understanding of human need and society comes into being. The result is a totalizing process. The past is seen as a romantic age that needs to be brought back to life. Or the present is romanticized as the path to total freedom. When in a dynamic tension, the past informs the present of possibilities achieved and/or squandered; the present values and learns from the past even as it seeks to move beyond what was. The middle of past and present ultimately gives birth to a future that includes and transcends both.

The brokenness found in the past and the present is added to this dynamic tension. Brokenness is inherent in life. It reminds us that those who propose the past or the present to overcome this brokenness are attempting to overcome the middle.

The great totalitarian movements of our time assume such a posture. To break through the broken middle, a messianic understanding of the world is projected as a way toward freedom. This understanding in thought and action is totalitarian; it seeks to strip tension, contradiction, and folly from the world. The broken middle seeks a more realistic sense of the world. It rejects complacency, as if limitations dominate the future. It also rejects hyperactivity, as if complete freedom is achievable.

Gillian sees the interplay between past and present in the context of thought. Upon reflection, I wonder if the broken middle also applies to events and the way we perceive them. Talking with Gillian at Auschwitz, I began to think of Jerusalem as the middle of Israel and Palestine. I wondered if the sharing of this middle can help us think through what we as Jews are doing.

Jerusalem is the middle in a variety of ways: as a historical symbol that both Jews and Palestinians hold dear; as a sacred city with religious landmarks important to both; as an economic and political city that helps ground both peoples. Jerusalem is also broken. As a city it has experienced great suffering and has sustained a cycle of violence through the millennia. Jews and Palestinians and the religions found among them—Judaism, Christianity, and Islam—have been conquerors and conquered. The graveyards around Jerusalem are full of those who conquered the city and were subsequently driven from it.

I wondered if this broken middle could reach beyond the discussions we were having at Auschwitz. This broken middle could take a directionless Auschwitz and place it in motion. The motion would be neither toward the past nor the present. The motion would be toward a shared future that connects aspects of history, peoples, and religions in a new configuration.

The broken middle of Jerusalem is neither a return nor a triumph. It is a place of mutual recognition of history and suffering. This might help us see Auschwitz as a place of unbelievable suffering *and* as a place from which a solidarity with others who have suffered must arise. Gillian and I spoke about healing Jews and Palestinians in the interplay of life in Jerusalem where both peoples meet symbolically and concretely.

The discussions at Auschwitz were abstract. The chasm between Auschwitz as it was and our lives today was too much. Even the dialectic of Auschwitz and Jerusalem becomes ephemeral. After visiting Jerusalem and Auschwitz, I realize that Jerusalem is not a response to Auschwitz or its overturning. It cannot be the answer to a suffering so extreme. No city can carry this weight. The attempt to have it do so leads to a further weight, the displacement of Palestinians throughout the land and in Jerusalem itself, which leads to further brokenness of both peoples.

In triumph, Jerusalem extends the era of Auschwitz. In the recognition of brokenness, the end of the era of Auschwitz comes into view. The broken middle allows the history of suffering and violence to be acknowledged. It opens the present to a dialogue about a future that is born from the past but is not limited to it. Tied to Auschwitz, Jerusalem's future is foretold, emerging from Auschwitz and the creation of Israel. In light of the catastrophe that has befallen the Palestinians, Jerusalem's future needs to be opened. I envision a shared Jerusalem as completing the narrative of Auschwitz in a way that moves toward healing.

The ramifications of sharing Jerusalem move far beyond the city itself. A shared Jerusalem admits that contemporary Jewish life is shared with others; that there are many peoples who have experienced brokenness in the recent past. There are many middles that Jews share with others.

In the West, the most obvious sharing is with Christians. The middle is the public life into which we have integrated into after the Holocaust. The brokenness is the shared bloody history we are now working through together. The ecumenical dialogue in the West anticipates the dialogue that could evolve among Jews and Palestinians. If Jews can live among Christians in the West after the Holocaust, it is more than possible for Jews and Palestinians to live together after their relatively recent experience of enmity.

In our final deliberations as a delegation, I wondered about this last point. Integration in the West has been achieved. Though our memory is one of suffering, our contemporary experience is just the opposite. As Gillian commented, we hardly took notice of the suffering around us in Poland. The suffering of Palestinians was a forbidden topic.

Perhaps sharing Jerusalem is the other side of allowing Auschwitz to fade in memory and to nature's decay. The protection of Auschwitz in memory and place needs Jerusalem as a Jewish capital and a symbol of triumph. A cycle ensues. The Holocaust needs protection from the accusing images of the present, as does Jerusalem. The Holocaust needs protection from the ongoing process of history, as does Israel. Both Auschwitz and Jerusalem assume a status outside of history. They become symbols to be called upon, but without direction or evolution. Discussing Auschwitz and Jerusalem in terms of history, in comparison with other events of death, or even in comparative studies of the evolution of cities with multicultural pasts and futures, is seen as dangerous.

If the broken middle is affirmed in the Middle East, it could become articulate in the lives we lead in America. So could the consequences. Assimilation would be discussed less with regard to intermarriage than in relation to power and justice. The delegates would respond to those who continue to experience alienation and poverty in America. Lifted out of innocence, the broken middle that Jews are living within would be analyzed in detail.

African Americans, for example, experience the integration of Jews in America in a decidedly mixed way. Jewish suffering in the European past is a gateway to status in America as the historical past and present of racism continues to affect the African American community. Often African Americans experience the Holocaust as a shield against their own aspirations, as if their suffering in the Americas, then and now, is trivial compared to Jewish suffering during the Nazi era. Often the way we remember the Holocaust signals an unannounced alignment with the white power structure in America.

In the end, the broken middle of Jerusalem may be no more threatening than the broken middle of Washington. To hold on to Auschwitz, as if we own it, is to hold on to America, as if it is the promised land. In this scenario, the Polish people, Palestinians, African Americans, Latinos, and others take a back seat. They are simply a backdrop for a larger and more significant drama.

One can look at the Holocaust narrative in the West as a public liturgy that is grateful for the place of rescue even as it laments its previous isolation in the same culture. A claim is staked on the West and Christianity: guilt for previous disenfranchisement, gratitude for a new alliance. What of those who continue to be displaced by the culture Jews now celebrate? Can they question us in a provocative way, suggesting that we have made the same deal that others made under which Jews suffered?

The delegates did not analyze Auschwitz as a place from which critical thought about contemporary Jewish experience could arise. They were, in a manner of speaking, stuck in Auschwitz, ideologically and symbolically for a lifetime, physically for only a week. They did not embark on a process of healing because it is simply too dangerous.

What does fidelity for Jews mean in the broken middle? What does it mean to be Jewish after Auschwitz *and* Israel, in America *and* in Israel? What do African Americans and Palestinians, and people who are poor and suffering around the world, say to Jews when we remember Auschwitz? When we use the Holocaust as a shield and a protector, avoiding the broken middle or allying ourselves with unjust power?

What does the memory of Auschwitz mean for those Jews who have crossed over into the broken middle in solidarity with those who are suffering? How is this memory to be articulated and to whom will it make sense? Is there to be a Jewish memory of Auschwitz or will it one day become a memory for all people ?

These are the questions I took with me from Auschwitz.

✥

THREE YEARS after I met Gillian Rose at Auschwitz, she died of cancer. I had met her twice after our journey to Auschwitz. The first time was in New York City, when she came to bury her teacher, who had recently died of AIDS. The last time was in England, where she was on the faculty at the University of Warwick. All in all I had spent only about ten days in her company and yet she had a profound effect on my life.

In some ways Gillian reminded me of Simone Weil, a French Jew who was very attracted to Christianity in a mystical and complex way. Like Weil, Gillian was brilliant, engaging, difficult, and stubborn. Both were great intellectuals.

Yet she was also warm and tender. Gillian stayed on at Auschwitz for a few days after I left for America. She had to move to another hotel and I volunteered to help her. I remember standing in the stairwell looking down at the ground as I picked up her oversized, heavy bag. I noticed that her shoes were untied and I thought for a second of simply dropping to the floor and tying them. Gillian was somehow divorced from her own physicality, or so it seemed. There was a certain vulnerability, almost helplessness about her. I had the sense that she was quite able to take care of herself and unable at the same time. Her exterior was somewhat cold. Her vulnerability was hidden. It was also appealing.

Her death was a difficult one. It stretched on for almost two years and engaged her mother, Lynn, in a frantic attempt to save her life and then to comfort her as her death became imminent.

Much had happened since the last time I saw Gillian. The Oslo agreements were signed. Rabin was assassinated. The fiftieth anniversary of the liberation of the death camps had been commemorated.

On that anniversary, Elie Wiesel wrote poignantly of his arguments with God and the need for reconciliation. In spite of his quarrel with God, Wiesel had never lost his faith. He had only suppressed and whispered it because of his loss. For Wiesel, Auschwitz was a human invention. Murder was planned and carried out by human beings. Still Auschwitz could hardly be understood apart from God. God had a responsibility to protect Jews. God experienced pain in seeing the Jewish people suffering so much.

In her last days Gillian also reconciled herself with God. She did so through conversion to Christianity. For many in the philosophical world, Gillian's conversion came as quite a surprise. This great philosopher had crossed a boundary that few Jews had the inclination or courage to cross. As a public figure of some note in Europe, her conversion was alluded to in some obituaries. In other accounts of her life's work it was emphasized.

Gillian's memoir, *Love's Work,* was published just months before her death. In one chapter she recalls her journey to Auschwitz and the anger and distance she felt there. Gillian identified with the Polish people she met and the Jews who had died. She objected to the role of the delegation and the delegates that surrounded her. "What vain posturing! Scientific status, superimposed on the even more dubious notions of cerebral and cultural ethnic identity!" Gillian wrote. "We were set up. Enticed to preen ourselves as *consultants,* in effect our participation was staged. Conscripted to restructure the meaning of 'Auschwitz,' we were observed rather than observing, the objects of continuous Holocaust ethnography, of Holocaust folk law and lore."

Gillian understood Jews as a martyred people. The Polish people were also martyred. In World War II and at Auschwitz as well, Poland

suffered occupation, destruction, and death. The convent controversy, which resulted from a Carmelite order erecting crosses at
Auschwitz, so animated the years previous to our visit that it brought
the controversy over martyrdom to a head. Is Auschwitz a symbol for
Jews or for Poles? The appearance of a large cross facing the camp
right outside the spot considered to be the historical boundary of
Auschwitz raised this war over symbols to an international level. The
claims on Auschwitz were mutual.

Gillian recognized the separation of the Jewish and Polish experiences *and* their commonality. She asked if there is a way to see both
in their particularity and commonality. If her sensibility had been
adopted it might have motivated the delegation to meet the Polish
people around us in the present as a struggling people. Instead, the
delegation avoided and sometimes caricatured them as anti-Semitic
murderers.

Conversion to another religion is difficult to understand from the
outside. It is no less difficult to describe from the inside. Gillian's
conversion may simply have been an embrace of a mystical and life-
changing experience she had. No doubt there are many factors involved. Her conversion may have been the discovery of a way forward
where she saw none in Jewish life. Surely Gillian sought an embrace
that involved God and humanity where she had previously experienced distance and separation.

Her memoirs are short and schematic. The majority of her memoirs recall her experience at Auschwitz and the illness and death of
her teacher from AIDS. Both involve past events of meaning. A second part of her memoir is reflection on the present; defining
Auschwitz and the terrible situation of abandonment in which she
found her teacher.

Working through these experiences is what Gillian called "love's
work." Love's work is being attentive to the changing contexts of personal and communal life in a solidarity that is informed and compas-
sionate. Love's work is self-critical, aware of and involved in the work
of the world. "For politics does not happen when you act on behalf of
your own damaged goods," Gillian wrote, "but when you act, *without
guarantees*, for the good of all—that is to take *the risk* of the *universal* interest." It may be this understanding of politics transposed to
religion that forced Gillian's hand. She found contemporary Judaism
wanting.

When I first heard Gillian speak of caring for her dying friend, I thought of Etty Hillesum. Etty was a German-Dutch Jew in her twenties when she volunteered to help her fellow Jews interned in Westerbork. Westerbork was a transit camp for Jewish refugees crossing into the Netherlands in the early years of the Nazi regime. When the Nazis invaded the Netherlands, the number of inmates swelled. Then the Dutch Jews were also interned. They awaited transit to the East. Unbeknownst to them, their destination was Auschwitz.

Despite her ability to leave for safety, Etty accompanied her family and community to their death in Auschwitz. Etty was a person who struggled to embrace the diversity she found within herself as a person and her inheritance as a Jew and a European. Her diaries, discovered after the war, are like Gillian's memoirs. They are filled with compassion and exploration, affirming a goodness in life despite the tragic elements within it.

Like Gillian, Etty was drawn to Christianity, though she never embraced it formally. Etty was drawn to the spirituality in the Bible as well as in European literature and philosophy. As the crisis of European Jewry deepened, she defined herself more explicitly as a Jew. She also expanded the diversity of her reading and experiments with spirituality. Etty came to see the embrace of her Jewishness as an act, in Gillian's words, "without guarantees," as a risk taken in a "universal interest." Though her personal safety was endangered, Etty saw that danger as a witness to a world arising after the Holocaust. Her identification as a Jew was one of solidarity.

This solidarity was contemporary with other Jews but also with non-Jews who were suffering. Solidarity in the present meant accompanying others in their suffering, regardless of creed or ethnicity. Aware of the past, immersed in the present, Etty's solidarity was given freely as a witness to a future created out of the ashes of destruction.

Etty did her love's work in Westerbork and in Auschwitz without attachment, a sense of uniqueness, or even, at least according to her diaries, thoughts about the future of Jewish life. *The future is to be shared and her witness as a Jew is to a broader humanity, a humanity under assault.* This is the message that the delegates at Auschwitz had forgotten.

Etty's "conversion" lay in her caring for others and allowing the horror of the Holocaust to give birth to a future that she would not control. The future comes from brokenness and hope, from a middle that does not try to romanticize or escape suffering. Etty's conversion was a commitment to do love's work in the concentration camps and to hope that others continue that work in the reconstruction of Europe after the war.

I think of Gillian and Etty together. Are they lost to the Jewish world because of their interest in Christianity? Or did both explore the boundaries of Jewish life in their own day and find them wanting? Perhaps they stumbled upon a path within Jewish life that has been declared off-limits, the path that grew from Judaism and became Christianity. Perhaps they both found a more inclusive spiritual geography necessary for them to embrace the brokenness of their time.

Gillian witnessed at Auschwitz what Etty experienced within it. They both found that the spiritual resources emerging from the death camps are beyond the capacity of one tradition to handle. Most of the delegates were "stuck" at Auschwitz because they had no capacity to move beyond it. Gillian and Etty attempted to move beyond the era of Auschwitz. Mainstream Jewish life sees them as renegades and traitors.

Many Jews today cross boundaries into Buddhism, new age spirituality, and a secularization that today is almost complete. They, too, attest to the failure of owning Auschwitz. Conversion should be seen in a broader category. On the one hand, conversion is an attempt to escape a dead end. On the other hand, it is an attempt to expand the possibilities of embrace and commitment. Conversion seeks a foundation to do love's work. Those who cross boundaries ask whether the lessons of the Holocaust relate primarily to religious affiliation or to establishing values that create a new world out of the broken middle. In that world to come, the primary identifier is not Judaism or Christianity. It is the values one embodies and transmits.

There are disciplines that make sense in light of Auschwitz and Israel and help individuals and communities become "unstuck." What are those disciplines? Do they allow us to continue on within our context, always moving toward a place beyond it as well? If there is a tangible broken middle, like the city of Jerusalem, is there a theological broken middle as well? What are the boundaries that need to be crossed and are there new ones to be created? Do these new disciplines seek to establish themselves as new orthodoxies, or are they fluid, always changing and ready to be embraced and let go of?

◒

MY FEELING IS that Gillian and Etty represent a dialogue across geography and time that is buried in contemporary Jewish life. The attraction to Christianity, or rather the elements within Christianity with which Gillian and Etty identified, is one aspect of this dialogue. Are these elements "Christian" in their origin? Are they "owned" by Christianity like the Holocaust is "owned" by Jews? Did Gillian or Etty embrace a Christianity that is actually practiced by Christians, or did they explore elements in the Christian tradition that for the most part are not practiced by Christians?

What is lacking in Judaism that leads spiritual seekers elsewhere? The losses have been great in the Holocaust *and* in the owning of the Holocaust. In coming to grips with the memory of dislocation and death *and* in the causing of dislocation and death, Jews are propelled outward. Witnesses to a diverse and open spirituality are, for the most part, unknown in the Jewish world—or derided. If it is impossible to speak in a positive way about the French survivors who came by train to Auschwitz and developed their own way of commemorating their experience, how can one mention the spirituality of Etty Hillesum who died in Auschwitz?

Much of the discussion by the delegates at Auschwitz concerned the desecration at the site. Included in this definition were European teenagers who volunteered to work at Auschwitz for the summer. As a gesture of solidarity with the victims, they fashioned crosses out of wood and erected them on the grounds where the crematorium stood. Some of the delegates were furious and complained that the crosses violated the dead and living Jews as well. They demanded that the crosses be removed immediately. I wonder what the delegates thought when a group of Jewish Buddhists held a retreat at Auschwitz in 1997 to come to terms with this tragedy by sitting in silence.

Surely, the geography of embrace has been narrowed as the Jewish world has been militarized. What is outside the Jewish tradition?

The tradition I inherit has diverse centers and perspectives. Do we now stop the evolution of Jewish life? Gillian Rose and Etty Hillesum, like those who are drawn to Buddhism and other religions, are part of the ongoing evolution and expansion of Jewish sensibility. They search for a discipline requisite to the time in which we live.

Since the center of Jewish life today revolves around the Holocaust and Israel, it is important to identify other parts of the tradition that might become centers in the future. Through this exploration a broken middle can emerge. Important Jewish thinkers come readily to mind. In the present, Noam Chomsky, the linguist and political analyst who grew up in a working-class Jewish culture, is a binationalist Zionist. Today he is one of the foremost experts on world affairs. From the past, the names of Karl Marx, Sigmund Freud, and Hannah Arendt come readily to mind.

What I find interesting in these latter figures is how widespread their contribution is and how often they are embraced by others in the world, and sometimes by Jews, as if their European identity explained their background and the foundation from which their thought sprang. Freud is a prime example of this confusion. Freud's father was a lay Talmudic scholar. On Freud's thirty-fifth birthday, his father gave him the family Bible as a present. It was the Bible Freud studied as a child and his father's inscription, written in Hebrew, is filled with biblical allusions. It begins naturally enough with Freud's Hebrew name, Shlomo. In the Nazi years Freud was driven from Vienna. Much of his immediate family was lost in the Holocaust. Yet when Freud is studied, his Jewishness is rarely discussed. He becomes a European in general.

By the time of the Holocaust, the religious center was challenged. Orthodox practice had already ceased to define what it meant to be Jewish. There was a dynamic explosion of perspectives and possibilities in Jewish life that featured an exploration of boundaries and the crossing of them. The middle was exciting and challenging. This continued in many ways after the Holocaust. But the definition of Auschwitz and Israel as the litmus test for Jewish identification has defined the evolving middle as outside the tradition. *Thus retroactively and in the present those who explore and cross the boundaries of Jewish life before and after the Holocaust and Israel—those who refuse the definition of a center that is aligned with the state and has no direction—are expelled from the Jewish world.* It is little wonder that those with different models of exploration choose to explore else-where. These become the "only" Jews I meet everywhere I travel.

The gathering of these Jews renders conversion, in the traditional sense of leaving behind one tradition to embrace another, obsolete. Because of the traditional definition of conversion we are left with the delegates at Auschwitz or with those who seek to renew the tra-dition through return to symbols and texts that have lost their power to create a way of life. The tradition itself can only make sense if the movement of those who have and continue to cross boundaries can be seen in a broader tradition of faith and struggle.

The middle we are struggling toward can be found within and be-yond what is known as Judaism and Jewish life. There is a much broader geography of embrace necessary to Jews and others as the twenty-first century dawns. This geography must no longer be de-fined, always and everywhere, as foreign, especially when it has been bequeathed by Jewish history and Jews themselves.

7
Martyrdom

I HAD ALREADY TRAVELED WIDELY before my visit to Auschwitz. My opportunity for travel came through my employment as a professor at the Maryknoll School of Theology. Maryknoll is a Catholic missionary order with mission sites in Latin America, Africa, and Asia.

Maryknoll is a fascinating place. It began in the 1920s as an American Catholic missionary effort to evangelize China. During the 1940s, some Maryknollers were imprisoned in China. Others spent those turbulent years in internment camps in the Philippines. With the victory of Mao's revolutionary forces, Maryknoll was expelled from China. This expulsion forced a dispersion and the discovery of new mission fields. Soon Maryknollers were in Hong Kong and other parts of Asia. Africa and Latin America also began to receive Maryknoll's attention. The 1950s was a time of tremendous growth in Catholic vocations to the priesthood. American Catholic religious orders grew rapidly. Maryknoll was no exception.

The school where I came to teach was originally a seminary. In the 1950s, the seminary was overflowing. A strict discipline was in force and infractions sometimes caused the postulant to be sent home for good. The missionary future was assured with Maryknoll the leading light. Full speed ahead.

Yet as the momentum was increasing, the world was changing. The Second Vatican Council was called and the winds of change were felt throughout the Catholic world. The wake of Vatican II cut in two directions, conservative and liberal. In the end, a serious split in the Catholic Church occurred. Though over time many progressive priests would leave their orders, the initial exodus was of more traditional priests who could not adjust to the changing church. By the time I arrived in 1980, the seminary was almost empty. Vocations, once so plentiful, were drying up. The average age of the Maryknoll priests was increasing. The signs were everywhere and even reported in the Maryknoll internal newspaper. In the coming decades, Maryknoll, as an institutional vocational order of the Catholic Church, would change or die.

Maryknoll is caught between its missionary past, which emphasized conversion in the traditional sense, and its present, where the inheritance of the peoples they serve is more respected. Many of the priests of Maryknoll retain their conception of the center of Catholicism as the one true way of salvation. Others are caught in the middle of this debate between converting and respecting others as a way of learning and sharing life together. The confines of the missionary tradition itself make it difficult for a middle to emerge. As a missionary order within the Roman Catholic tradition, Maryknoll is sometimes, and in a fascinating way, stuck.

I had arrived at Maryknoll in an unexpected way. A member of the Maryknoll governing board, Gene Toland, read my reflections on my stay at the Catholic Worker. It is a typical Maryknoll story—with a twist. Traveling to the Middle East to find a place for Maryknoll's first mission center among Muslims, Gene bought a copy of my book in a New York bookstore and carried it with him to the Middle East. He read it in an airport in Saudi Arabia as he awaited a flight to Yemen. He was taken with the description of my life with the poor on the streets of the Bowery in New York City and compared it with his previous experience with the poor in Bolivia. Gene wrote me a letter about this and, since he did not know of my whereabouts, he sent it to my publisher, who forwarded it to me.

I received the letter at Marquette University where I was finishing my doctorate under the supervision of William Miller, the historian of the Worker movement and the biographer of Dorothy Day. When I received the letter I hardly knew what to think. An unsolicited letter sent from Saudi Arabia was a surprise. A letter from a Catholic missionary priest who had worked among the poor in Latin America and now wanted to create dialogue with Muslims in the Middle East was also a surprise. The combination was intriguing.

I responded to his New York address and soon I was visiting Maryknoll at the community's invitation. After fifteen minutes in the dean's office, he offered me a teaching position. It was so quick, I didn't know what to do. Did he mean a full-time job? Did he remember that I am Jewish? With the seminary numbers down, Maryknoll wanted to expand the seminary's constituency and transform it into a school of theology. Gene thought I could help in this endeavor.

Several months later I was teaching in an environment that, before my visit, I did not know existed. Maryknoll is a world unto itself, a culture across cultures, a global network of travel and commitment.

My arrival at Maryknoll was accompanied by a dramatic event. Two Maryknoll sisters, Ita Ford and Maura Clark, and a lay worker trained at Maryknoll, Jean Donavan, were murdered in El Salvador. The context of the murders was the country's civil war in a larger region convulsed by war. A revolution in Nicaragua had just taken place and the United States government, along with conservative elements in the region, was determined to overturn the revolution. They feared that other countries might take the same path.

Thousands of people were killed yearly in Central America during the 1980s. Those who carried out Christian education and missionary work were considered subversive by forces aligned with the right-wing factions in power or attempting to return to power. The three Maryknoll women worked among the poor and tried to help them survive the civil war in El Salvador. For this they were deemed subversive. Their murder was a warning to the part of the church that identified itself with the poor.

These religious women were immediately labeled martyrs. The church services emphasized that these women had died for their faith. Why else would they be among the poor in a foreign country? They became missioners because of their faith. They were martyrs because they remained in El Salvador despite the danger and because in their deaths they witnessed to the importance of the Christian faith.

To whom do they witness? Surely to others who make similar commitments in El Salvador and other countries beset by violence. They witness to faith by remaining faithful until death. That witness was made explicit by those who gave the sermons at the memorial services. Still, the overall context for remembering these women is within the Catholic tradition and the central ritual of that tradition, the Mass. Here their service is to God, mediated by Jesus. They died for him as he had died for them. They returned to Jesus in their deaths and now are witnesses to the life, death, and resurrection modeled by him.

Do they also witness to me as a Jew? Out of respect, I attended the Masses and felt the power of a community remembering its own. There was a tremendous humility on the part of the Maryknoll community leaders. They emphasized that the Maryknoll women were known and accorded respect in their deaths because they were affiliated with a religious congregation and because they were from the United States.

But the poor are without connection and their burial site is often an anonymous grave. Certainly the cameras and news media were absent from the memorial Masses for the poor while the deaths of the American religious women became national news. The Maryknollers' deaths intensified the ongoing debate about United States support for the repressive Salvadoran government. Still, as I sat through the ceremonies and listened to other Maryknollers recall their murdered friends, I felt outside, as if their martyrdom did not speak to me.

Was it the language of the Mass itself that made me feel like an outsider? The insistence that all should celebrate their resurrection? The almost pristine way they were remembered? The language of the liturgy almost replaced their lives and the horror of their deaths. I felt that the the Catholic tradition had difficulty handling death *as death* and needed to invent another category.

I wondered if their deaths should speak to me and what language could accomplish this. Surely the Catholic tradition had difficulty making sense of the peculiar transposition that these women represent. They died for justice in opposition to unjust power often carried out in the name of the very same religion they claimed. Their lives were so brutally ended because they showed solidarity with those who are suffering. But it was almost as if they had to be fit back into a compartment that Christians could understand. I wondered if they had entered a different level of experience that needs a broader field for explaining and making sense of their deaths. Is their fidelity summed up in the Catholic ritual and Christian faith?

Beyond the Mass a battle was being waged for the heart of Catholicism and Christianity in general. As much as these women were victims of a government, they were also victims of a division within Christianity that has widened in the years since. They tended to the masses of poor and indigenous people who had historically suffered from the arrival of Christianity. Christianity accompanied the conquistadors, aligned with the power of the king. Now it was aligned with the power of the state. The assimilation of Christianity into the state, an assimilation now over a thousand years old, was the center of Christianity from which the Maryknoll order was simply an extension. Part of the church and part of Maryknoll were now refusing that assimilation.

The women died in the cycle that Christianity helped introduce in the Americas. On the one hand, they died as testimony to their faith as Christians. On the other hand, the very tradition that labeled them martyrs was also partly responsible for their deaths. Is their testimony now enfolded in the Christianity they died within and for? Does the overall thrust of the tradition remain more important to the institution than their witness? Would their witness strengthen Christianity and lead again to another cycle of violence once their witness was forgotten or safely canonized?

I grew up with the understanding of martyrdom as ancient and contemporary. The stories of Rabbi Akiva being hacked to death by the Romans in the first century as he recited the Sh'ma are vivid from childhood. Those who died in the Holocaust are often referred to as martyrs, though the stories of their deaths are typically less individualized.

Akiva was a martyr because he chose death rather than accept religious coercion. The term *martyr* relating to the Holocaust is less clear to me. That lack of clarity surfaced again in the wake of the murder of these religious women. Are they more like Akiva, individuals who said no to power? Or are they more like the victims of the Holocaust, since behind them are so many dead? Perhaps they are related to both and different also, because their deaths came from a commitment and were in the context of a people. Is the major difference, articulated in the Mass, that they died for their belief in Jesus the messiah, the same belief that Jews refuse? Here I find a similarity that must be noted. The force that killed the women and the Jews is tied to Christianity.

Martyrdom is witness. I wonder if there a similarity among martyrs across time, geography, and religious affiliation. Do martyrs witness to each other? I wonder if they join in a tradition of martyrdom because it provides a meaning that the religious traditions are no longer able to articulate.

If martyrs are seen within a broader tradition of faith and struggle, then the limitations and possibilities of liturgical expression and critical thought can be expanded. In their brokenness and hope, a middle emerges. I see martyrs of all peoples, those who chose death and those who had no choice, together.

Beneath the politics and the violence of civil war and atrocity lies the desire of people for an ordinary life—the ability to live and love, raise children, work, and worship. As I sat at the Masses and later at Auschwitz, I thought this simple fact joined those who suffered and died anonymously and those who became known to the world in their commitment until death. The continuum is the desire and fight for the ordinary, its denial, and the attempt to restore it. The accusation made by some politicians in El Salvador and in the United States that the involvement of the religious women in politics was wrong, at least, in the traditional meaning of politics. Rather than power or public policy, they witnessed to the right to ordinary life for the citizens of a country.

In their minds they were ordinary women of faith. Their practice of faith is a discipline: one that evolves, sometimes fails, and other times brings hope. The people they served in El Salvador were in many respects similar to the Jews who were displaced and murdered in Europe. As human beings, Jews and Salvadorans desire and deserve ordinary life for themselves and their families. Behind the horrible specter of death in the Holocaust was the stripping away of dignity, the humiliation of the individual and a people. Those who died in the Holocaust and those who survived as refugees were brutally ripped from the ordinary cadences of life. Without the ordinary, how is meaning to be searched for and found?

Martyrs are those who are aware that the humiliation of the person and a people leads to a void of possibility and meaning. Therefore, it must be fought against in the most ordinary of ways: by bringing food to the hungry and solace to the humiliated.

Within atrocity the restoration of the ordinary is impossible. Therefore, the deeds of the anonymous and the known fail. The designation of martyrdom is a retrospective act that tries to heal the void that opens in the course of history. The void is the same for those who experience it and the designation of martyrdom is the same for the community that survives it. There is a commonality of the experience of atrocity and martyrdom.

For communities that suffer humiliation and death, their lives can never be the same. The glorification of martyrs cannot explain or heal the wounds. *Neither the Masses nor the silence at Auschwitz is enough to heal the wounds of atrocity and create a new ordinary. The people are never the same, nor is God.* It is an illusion to think that a way forward can be found only within the community that has suffered or only within a shared religious affiliation.

In their deaths the women had a future well beyond the confines of the church that celebrated their ascension to God. I wonder whether that is also true of the victims of Auschwitz. They too, have a future in death beyond the Jewish community that claims them.

꿏

I LEFT for an extensive tour of Latin America several months after the murders. There I witnessed the struggle of individuals and peoples to restore an ordinary life for their families and communities.

I traveled to Chile, where a long history of democracy ended in a military coup in 1973 with the aid of the United States. When I visited there, people were attempting to survive the dictatorship and slowly move back in the direction of democracy. The struggle against the military dictatorship was clandestine and the church served as an institutional buffer between the government and the people. I met with priests in the church hierarchy and activists who camouflaged their resistance to the dictatorship. I was disappointed when after my visit Pope John Paul II served communion to Augusto Pinochet, the Chilean dictator.

I also visited a small town outside Santiago. We stopped at the home of a parishioner. Her surroundings were poor by almost any standard. The frame of the house was wooden but unevenly finished. Plastic covered the openings. Inside the furnishings were sparse; the floor lacked a foundation. When I was introduced by the priest, he told her that I taught at Maryknoll and that I was Jewish. I had no idea of whether the women had ever met a Jew or what she might think of Jews. She immediately exclaimed: "Another way to God!" I was humbled by her comment and her sophistication.

The struggle in Peru was somewhat different. Large numbers of indigenous people retained their culture and fought to have this recognized in the political and cultural life of the country. For most of my visit I stayed in the home of a Maryknoll missionary on the outskirts of Lima. The landscape was littered with garbage and populated by the poor. The garbage and the poor were treated by society almost identically. During my visit I saw another Maryknoll priest baptize a child dying of starvation.

Nicaragua was also different. Nicaragua is an incredibly poor country and its recent revolution held promise for the future. This, too, was fought against. Within Nicaragua the privileged and the wealthy sought to counter the revolution. Parts of the church that identified with the privileged also opposed it. The United States government saw the revolution as somehow a threat to its national security. Here I visited a number of lay missionaries I had recently taught at Maryknoll. Some worked with small Christian communities to communicate their concerns and needs to the government. Others worked as translators and press people, using the media to describe the revolution to the outside world. Revolutionary murals were everywhere, and often as not the struggle of the people was depicted with Christian symbolism.

In each of these countries the church was split. Some within society and the church supported the exercise of power against movements for change. Others organized in solidarity with the poor. Nicaragua was the most obvious in this regard. It had a church establishment that opposed the revolutionary government and several priests, including a Maryknoller, in the highest levels of the government. Shortly after my visit the Pope publicly chastised the noted priest and poet Ernesto Cardenal for his support of the revolution and his duties as Minister of Cultural Affairs in the government. Until the end of the Sandinista period, Maryknoll was constantly pressured to persuade one of its priests, Miquel d'Escoto, to resign his government post. Apparently, priests should not meddle in politics. But this hint was made at the same time that the Pope was engaged in intense political work to help liberate Poland from its Soviet orbit.

Cardenal is representative of liberation theology, a theology that developed in Latin America in the 1960s and 1970s in response to the increasing gap between the wealth of the few and the impoverishment of the many. Yet sometimes I find in the theological world a gross distortion of the theology and the people involved in it. One distortion is the supposed politicization of theology. But Cardenal belied this superficial characterization. He had been a disciple of Thomas Merton in the 1960s and lived some years at Gethsemani, Merton's monastery. After a time of struggle and doubt, Merton advised Cardenal that his vocation was outside the monastery. He returned to his native Nicaragua and became a priest.

Eventually he went to Solentiname, an archipelago in the southern part of Lake Nicaragua. Cardenal lived among the villagers. During the Mass he would often invite their commentary on the New Testament readings. Their insights into the life of faith and the New Testament fascinated Cardenal and he began to record them. After some time, they were published as a series titled *The Gospel in Solentiname*.

Maryknoll's publishing house, Orbis, translated and published these volumes and I read them before I left for my trip to Latin America. They are haunting in their beauty and in their revolutionary fervor. The commentators are peasants who struggle for their daily bread. They see in the Gospels a manual for liberation. The parables of Jesus are taken in a much more literal sense than I was accustomed to reading in theological texts. The politics of Jesus' trial and death are taken to heart. They too are in a struggle, perhaps unto death, to establish justice. The kingdom of God is neither abstract or distant; it is to be struggled for in revolution.

The first articulation of that theology was in Peru, where the Peruvian priest Gustavo Gutiérrez wrote of the need for theology to be liberated from its support of unjust systems of power. Responding to the challenge of the Gospels, Gutiérrez called on Christians and the church to align themselves with the poor. Gutiérrez's first book, *A Theology of Liberation*, was also translated and published by Orbis. I read this along with the Solentiname commentaries. Cardenal is a poet and his rendering of the dialogues he had with the villagers is poetic. Gutiérrez is a theologian whose analysis is rigorous and bold.

Gutiérrez finds that the universal nature of Christianity and the sense that all Christians are united by a faith beyond history belies a division within both society and the church. When looked at sociologically, the church is as divided as society. In Latin America, those who have access to wealth and power are the few. Those who have neither are the great majority. The church and its theology posit a unity in faith, but when contradicted in the life of society, Gutiérrez finds "unity" to be a cover for disunity. The challenge of the church and theology is to take sides in this disunity as part of their struggle to be faithful to the poor and the suffering. Gutiérrez's fidelity is found within a concept of God and Jesus as being in solidarity with the poor.

Liberation theology grew from its introduction in the 1960s to become a force in politics just a decade later. The Nicaraguan revolution had many practitioners of liberation theology in its ranks and the religious women murdered in El Salvador were seen as representatives of the liberating church. In my travels I met with theologians in Nicaragua and elsewhere in Latin America. I also met with poor people who formed the base communities that brought liberation theology to life. I first read liberation theology at Maryknoll in New York. In Latin America it came boldly alive.

The people who live within the liberation framework are poor or working class. They struggle for what I take for granted—the right to full citizenship, water, food, and education, as well as respect for their culture and religion. The ideological and theological wars between the representatives of the right and the left in society and the church are beyond their scope and concern. Poor people want their children to reach adulthood, to be respected, and to flourish. They want an ordinary life within their country and among their people.

Who can argue with this desire, a desire so far from the world revolution feared by conservative commentators and politicians in the United States? How can the desire for sewers and clean water, for schools and homes, be translated into such a fantasy by those who have all of these in abundance? Why is the church, with the Gospels it reads and preaches, divided against the fulfillment of this desire?

The church traditionally dispensed charity. Now the call is for justice. Does the church fear that if justice is achieved the role of the church will diminish or even disappear? Perhaps the church fears persecution by those who seek to stop change. Why, then, raise up martyrs? Does the church fear what it preaches?

There were other disturbing dimensions of the situation in Latin America that I became more aware of as I left the continent. As an American, I know that my government is deeply responsible for many of these conditions among the poor. Even more disturbing is the realization that Israel is also deeply involved.

While the United States has overwhelming power in the Americas, Israel also acts as a surrogate power there. The divisions in the United States over the policies of the Reagan administration in the 1980s were often circumvented by Israel. Much of the training and military arms for those who fought the Nicaraguan government were supplied by Israel. In the 1970s and 1980s, Israel became the foremost supplier of arms and training to the forces of repression in El Salvador and Guatemala. This training included lessons and support for the torture and death squads that inundated the region during that period.

The power that sought to crush the aspirations of the people came from internal elites, elements of the church, America, and Israel. A segment of the Jewish elite in America helped as well. During this time a concerted effort to demonize liberation theology was begun. Enlisted, among others, were Jews who accused liberation theologians of twisting the Hebrew Bible to support their interests and of interpreting the Christian Gospels in an anti-Jewish way. At least in the minds of some Jews, liberation theology is affiliated with movements that support the Palestinian cause.

Because the United States is often cited by liberation theologians as wielding abusive economic and military power, they are also branded as anti-American. In wanting the role of the United States diminished and its interventionism curtailed, some Jewish leaders see liberation theology as a threat to Israel. If the United States turns inward and refuses a global military policy, will it still feel it is necessary to guarantee Israel's survival? Or will Israel be seen as a burden? A politicized theology coming from those who are suffering can therefore be seen as threatening Jewish interests. Hence, the dire warning that a prophetic stand for justice for the Palestinians or for justice movements around the world is dangerous to Israel. A prophetic identification with the suffering in the Middle East, in Latin America and beyond, could threaten the power and willingness of the United States to protect Israel. It might create the context for another Holocaust.

A conspiratorial worldview comes into being. Jewish identification with movements of social change are strictly monitored by the Jewish establishment. Theology challenging the power that serves the interests of the Jewish community *in its assimilation into power and the state* is defined as anti-Jewish. Jews who support these movements for justice are seen as undermining the security of Jews in Israel. If a revival of anti-Judaism in America takes place, being identified with justice movements might threaten the security of American Jews as well. Christians who seek to undo Jewish empowerment are labeled anti-Jewish. Their Jewish allies are labeled self-hating Jews.

In thinking through this worldview, I culled the following facts. The Jewish population of Latin America numbers less than 500,000. Two-thirds of that population is in Brazil and Argentina. Less than 10,000 Jews reside in all of Central America. Contemporary Judaism and Jewish life, including Israel, is almost never mentioned in liberation theology. Palestine and Palestinians are similarly absent. This does not dissuade the accusations of anti-Semitism and self-hate. The role of Israel as prime supplier of arms and training to oppressive and murderous movements and regimes is never mentioned by those Jews who attack liberation theology. The caution to "prophetic" Jews is rarely extended to those Jews who besmirch the memory of the Holocaust by helping to create a new event of atrocity committed on the bodies of the innocent.

A conundrum results. Jews who try to alleviate the suffering of the people do so because of the lessons of the Holocaust. These Jews also come from a people that now intellectually, politically, and militarily contributes to massive dislocation and death in Central and South America.

As I wandered around Managua, Nicaragua's capital city, I wondered how my own tradition had become ensnared in this conundrum. We have suffered and to end that suffering we seek empowerment. To become empowered we displace the Palestinian people. To defend that empowerment we build a strong and militarized Israel dependent on American financial aid and military guarantees. To keep in good stead with American power, and for its own financial benefit, Israel supplies arms and expertise to some of the most repressive regimes on earth. It assists those who seek to contain or overthrow movements for justice. Indigenous theologians who speak for peoples who have experienced historic and contemporary injustice and genocide are accused of being anti-Jewish on a continent where many of the few Jews who live there found refuge during and after the Nazi period. Those Jews who come into solidarity with those seeking an ordinary life are considered self-hating Jews.

For a Jew trying to be in solidarity with poor and struggling people the situation is almost hopelessly entangled. Nearly any expression of solidarity is seen as a form of betrayal. The inherent tendencies of my Judaism cannot be expressed without being suspect. An equally difficult reality came to the fore while I was in Latin America. I began to identify with Christians struggling for justice. I admired their commitment and their ability to express that commitment in religious terms.

◆

MY JOURNEY TO LATIN AMERICA was just the beginning of my travels through Maryknoll. By the time I arrived at Auschwitz, I had also been to parts of Africa and Asia and, of course, to the Middle East. I met and traveled with Muslims in Pakistan and Indonesia, Hindus in India, Buddhists in Korea and Japan, and people of many indigenous religions. Especially in Africa, most people seemed to combine world religions with their indigenous culture and religiosity. The theologians I met were mostly liberationists. They practiced their calling in diverse geographical and cultural contexts. Their job was difficult. Poverty was spreading and local and papal interference increased.

The media image of John Paul II is one of wisdom and contemplation. I witnessed another side of him as he disciplined church movements among the poor. I saw bishops and priests who supported the poor censored or transferred from their positions. Behind the pageantry of the Pope's many visits lies a church discipline that is rigorous and focused. In fact, many of the most harsh disciplines are enforced as the Pope's visits occur. The people remain poor and within the global economic system become even poorer as time goes on. The support for the poor that liberation theologians hoped to institutionalize is becoming increasingly distant.

Again I witnessed a serious contradiction. The attempt to make Christianity more responsive to local culture and more political on the side of the poor stretched the bonds of the Christian community. In local churches and in the broader world, so many people claim to be Christian that the very definition of what it means to be a Christian is elusive. If the bond of faith is defined as attending religious services and affirming Jesus as Lord, do movements of solidarity with the poor have anything to do with being Christian? If the poor and those who speak on their behalf claim that God is on their side in the struggle for freedom and dignity, does that mean that God is against those who have wealth and power even as they invoke God's name in ritual? Do those who speak of and work toward political change in the name of God and the church divide Christianity and blaspheme Jesus with their political agenda? Or is the church already divided?

By the 1990s, a new conservatism had entered the church. Liberation theology was on the defensive. I saw this on the faces of the theologians I visited. Gustavo Gutiérrez wrote boldly of the gospel call to justice in the 1960s and 1970s, as if the claims of theology, rooted in scripture and mandated by the savior Christians proclaimed, were clear. By the 1980s he wrote about Job and historical dissenters like the sixteenth-century priest Bartolomé de Las Casas.

Job was bewildered by his suffering and ended up on a dung heap. After rebelling, he accepted God's power and majesty without knowing God's plan of salvation. Las Casas was an early missionary in the Americas who protested the enslavement and deaths of the indigenous people. Like Job, Las Casas failed to stem injustice. Instead he stood as a witness to the truth of God. Both were faithful in their time, but their fidelity was to mystery and loss rather than revolution. The lesson of Job and Las Casas is clear: the poor can be defended; they do not experience justice or win their freedom.

Through Job, Gutiérrez proclaims that though he is humbled, he will not be silenced. Through Las Casas, Gutiérrez asserts that witness in history is more important than ecclesial politics. Gutiérrez proclaims this beautifully and hauntingly as his native Peru and Latin America enter a deeper cycle of poverty and violence.

I visited with Gutiérrez one afternoon in Lima and was tremendously impressed with the clarity of his vision. His spiritual depth is remarkable. A man of small physical stature, his wisdom is broad and encompassing. Rather than a firebrand, Gutiérrez is soft-spoken and deliberate in his responses to questions. After some time together, I wondered if he was beginning to recognize that the church would not commit itself to the liberation of the poor. Was he beginning to sense that the competition for the center of Christianity and its renewal had reached a dead end? That the institutional framework of the church and the claims of universality and transcendence of history made by Christianity had defeated the aims of liberation theology?

Gutiérrez, with others, wages a strategic battle to bring the institutional church into the struggle on behalf of the poor. As an institution with great moral and political power, the church can be a decisive asset in this struggle. In the end, however, the church often co-opts the message of liberation. The church betrays its own prophets.

Local churches and parts of the hierarchy may indeed respond to the poor. I witnessed this in my travels around the world. Still the battle is uneven. The resources that church and state bring to bear are overpowering and relentless. Martyrs multiply. This is why Gutiérrez writes hauntingly of the horrors of the Holocaust and the complicity of Christians in that horror. He also writes of the continuing slaughter on his native continent in which Christians again are complicit. Is he commenting on the end of Christian history as he has known and inherited it?

By the time I returned to Latin America in 1990, the conversation among liberation theologians had changed dramatically. The attempt at renewal was over. If some renewal had occurred in liturgy and outlook, the main thrust of liberation theology was diminished and sidelined. The acceptance of some of its ideas is part of this diminution. As these ideas and commitments are absorbed and placed in a broader, most often liturgical, framework they lose their force. Its revolutionary edge is blunted. Liberation theology is becoming a footnote to a larger Christian enterprise.

Some liberation theologians were persecuted by partisan segments of the church. One after another they were placed under investigation for their understandings of church dogma, brought to Rome, and silenced. Harassment takes its toll as the political and ecclesial authorities police theology. Death to some, hence the increasing number of martyrs, and the silencing of others who have spoken. Most important is the message that those thinking of traveling this path will pay a price. Censorship imposed from outside always encourages a far broader internal censorship.

Leonardo Boff, a liberation theologian from Brazil, was called to Rome in 1993 and silenced. He resigned his priesthood the following year and characterized the institutional church as closed and unrelenting. His carefully worded public statement hardly hid the meaning of his words. He had come to the end of Christianity.

8
Diaspora
in the Holy Land

DURING MY TRAVELS, a sense of connection emerged that helps clarify the disjointed experience of contemporary Jewish life. A world so seemingly divided between the pre- and post-Holocaust years merged into a continuum.

In terms of time, the Holocaust is near, just decades old. It ended just seven years before I was born. But the Jewish world has divided time as if the Holocaust stands alone. Contemporary victims of dislocation and death are seen at a distance.

My travels introduced a series of diverse connections that are difficult to make in a linear way. Nonetheless, they help place my inheritance in perspective. Though answers to the questions raised by the Holocaust remain elusive, contemporary struggles and theology—even their defeat and marginalization—focus what before was confusion.

Separated, Jews are observers of the present scene, without culpability or direct involvement. It is as though we live in the present without living here, as if our lives are assured without politics or exploitation. At Auschwitz, the delegates used this technique to divorce themselves from our surroundings, as though every Polish citizen could afford to fly across the ocean, stay in four-star hotels, and have meals flown in from Switzerland for religious dietary reasons. The reality is different. Few Polish people have the automobiles we take for granted, the spacious homes we own, or the prestige and security that accrue with university or rabbinic tenure.

From the Polish perspective, we were affluent and self-righteous people who could afford to dwell in memory and who used that memory as a form of separation. Once the connection between the past and the present is made, however, there is no turning back. Instead of being stuck in the Holocaust for our own sake, the call to reenter history in a conscious and critical way is compelling.

With this knowledge how do I proceed? For me, at least, I found the way in my travels to Israel and Germany. Over the years, I traveled to both countries, often in the same year, looking for a way forward. Israel, of course, is a response to the Holocaust, so that the linking of Israel and Germany is natural. Yet how one visits these countries and what one encounters often determines how the connection is established in the present.

In both Israel and Germany, I am constantly in a peculiar situation. I experience another dimension of history and time. Both countries are fraught with an overabundance of symbolism that makes it difficult to experience contemporary Israeli and German life as it is. History is found in every corner.

There are so many places where decisive events were discussed and dates when decisions were made. Cities like Berlin and Jerusalem carry a surfeit of despair and hope. If traveling to Berlin is returning to a dark page in Jewish history, Jerusalem is supposed to be turning that page. Berlin represents the power of decision that turned Auschwitz into a death camp. Jerusalem is the city from where the Holocaust is overturned and the destiny of the Jewish people fulfilled.

The places of both in my life were assured long before I went to either country. They were defined in symbolic terms before knowledge of history and contemporary context was even approached. Yet in traveling to these places of Jewish destiny, the reality is more complex. The Germany I visit contains the memories of the Nazi era and people struggling with them. It also has a complex life in the present, dealing with memory, and sometimes using that memory as a shield. Israel is also multilayered. I experience Israel as a modern society where memory has its place and, at the same time, is being displaced. There are accusing images in both countries—of the Holocaust in Germany and Palestinians in Israel. It is like being in a time machine that, while shuttling between past, present, and future, establishes a way of being in all three dimensions at once.

What I experience in Israel is the Holocaust and the Palestinians; Germany and Palestine; Judaism, Christianity and Islam; and the vast interplay of these events, countries, and religions. It was clear in my first trip to Israel in 1973, and even more vivid after visiting hospitalized Palestinian children in 1988, that Israel has incredible consequences for Jewish history. Israel is a reality rather than a dream or a theology. The continuous expansion of its borders occurs through the use of military force rather than through the force of Jewish ethics. The dream of Zion had a special role in the establishment of Israel. Now that dream is used to accomplish the dream of all states: affluence, stability, expansion, and consolidation of power. Israel uses memory and religion to legitimate these dreams.

Ordinary Israeli citizens pursue their lives as citizens of other countries might. They leave theology and philosophy to academics. As with most societies, Israel is divided between those who are affluent and those who are working class and poor. There is a color line in Israel as well, with Jews of European background being accepted and promoted as the norm of development and success. Jews of North African and Arab background are defined in relation to this norm. Predictably, the division of economic classes falls along this line of demarcation, as does educational achievement and access to political power. Those who languish in the jails of Israel are Jews disproportionately from North African and Arab background.

These simple and obvious facts startle the recent arrival who has been immersed in the shadow of the Holocaust and the dream of Israel. Israel aspires to a be a Western country in its form and development and is often analyzed as if it is located geographically in the West. Why then would these common divisions and problems be unexpected? Behind everything stands the Palestinian question. For many Jews, if Palestinians exist, they do so only at a distance as a menacing threat in time of war. Why then do these "invisible" people become visible?

At the time of the first Palestinian uprising I visited Palestinian hospitals and saw the children who had been shot by Israeli soldiers. Some would die, others would survive with paralysis or brain damage. What struck me was the helplessness of the children as they lay there in bed. Their parents and extended family tended to them as best they could. The doctors were unable to do much in the way of saving what had already been destroyed.

The hospitals were underfunded and under siege. Outdated and broken equipment was all around us. Blood for transfusions was in short supply. Often the ambulances that brought the children to the hospital had been delayed by Israeli security. Sometimes the hospitals were invaded by Israeli soldiers and searched for "terrorists." On some occasions patients were taken away. Their destination was unknown.

As martyrs for the Palestinian cause, the children were honored and their rooms covered with decorations symbolic of the Palestinian struggle. Often a picture of the child, enlarged and framed, hung behind the bed. Draped over the frame were kaffiyehs and flags with the colors of Palestine. Koranic verses were also displayed behind the child lying helplessly in bed. I was able to speak to some of the parents and the medical staff. At other times I was silent. I felt like weeping.

"God is great," the children outside the hospital shouted in Arabic as they began their demonstrations. Parents and Islamic religious leaders conversed during their visits. Yet for me the scene meant something other than a testimony of God's greatness. It meant the need to resist Jewish domination. It meant action to reestablish an ordinary life for Palestinians.

Were the Palestinians being crushed by soldiers that hate? Was this a Jewish payback for what had happened to us in another place and time? Male assertion where before we were emasculated? These reasons could account for the humiliation that was meted out by the soldiers. Reports abounded of the stripping of Palestinian males in public view, knocking on the doors to force the elderly to wash away the graffiti of the uprising, searching homes and bodies without dignity or restraint. I met Palestinians who had been tortured by Jewish soldiers. Their physical and psychological scars were visible. Some Palestinians appealed to me, questioned Jewish innocence, and sometimes compared Israelis to Nazis. I could only observe and listen.

After a visit to a Palestinian hospital in Jerusalem, a man who was along on the visit saw that I was visibly distraught. He took me aside and said the following: "I know that this probably won't help you now, but all occupation forces do these things, Jewish or not. They are agents of the state." Was this simply an exercise of occupying powers conducted across cultures and religions, bullets and humiliation to continue an occupation that a people resists? I immediately dismissed his words because for me these were agents of Jewish history. *We were becoming everything we loathed about our oppressors.*

Yet he was also partially right. The soldiers are agents of Jewish history *and* agents of the state. Over time the balance has shifted toward the state. I realized that the way for me to understand what was happening is to incorporate both aspects into a single vision. The challenge is the children *and* the soldiers, Jewish history *and* the state.

A confusion entered my mind and heart. Were the soldiers *my* soldiers, deserving of a solidarity that comes from a history and culture we share? Were the children *their* children, from a different history and culture? Or were they also, in the larger sense, *my* children? Did I identify with the soldiers or the children? The children's pillows were framed by tears and kaffiyehs. For whom was I crying, Jewish history or Palestinian suffering?

I asked what this joint history meant. Did it speak only of an embattled present, awaiting the time when the combatants can be separated? Did it speak also of a future of cooperation and mutuality? Did this joint history have theological ramifications? Was I traveling the diaspora in Israel and Palestine as I had in Latin America, Asia, and Africa?

I felt myself encountering a new expression of the diaspora within Israel and Palestine, or as I began to think of it, Israel/Palestine. I was encountering a division between Jews and Palestinians that one day would be overcome. I wondered if I would be drawn to Israel/Palestine as it evolved. Since I was not drawn to Israel as a state, it made little sense to be drawn to another state. Israel/Palestine would be more inclusive and just, to be sure, but a state nonetheless with all its imperatives and tendencies to embrace power as an end. One view of this coming together could be that of reconciliation and a shared destiny. This would represent a tremendous improvement over the situation I was witnessing.

Israel/Palestine would hardly be exempt from that which plagues all states. The structure of the state can provide the context for movements of justice and reconciliation. A hope for the future can come within it. Still the main business of forging a joint history occurs outside and beneath the policies of the state as it does with other states. *In thinking through Jewish history and the future of Israel/Palestine I found that a new diaspora was coming into being and that the link between the past and the creation of the future is the diaspora itself. This diaspora can only come into being with Jews and*

Palestinians forging a new bond and identity within and outside of the state.

What will this diaspora be and how will it affect Jews outside Israel/Palestine? To be a true diaspora in the context of the history created by Israel over the last decades, Palestinians inside and outside that state will also be affected. In a new state, both Jews and Palestinians inside *and* outside the land will embark on creating a new society; all will be welcome to return. Most Jews and Palestinians will not return, but a homeland will be in place for both.

Within Israel/Palestine, Jews and Palestinians in solidarity with their own people and with each other will find common interests and pursuits. Among them are religious and secular people and those who are neither religious or secular in the usual definition of the term. Coming from the Jewish, Muslim, and Christian traditions, all of which have been implicated in destruction and death in parts of the world, those in the broken middle of these traditions can voice a new religiosity. Because the center of the three faiths will be open and shared, those from the other diasporas around the world might also be influenced by what happens there. The influence will be mutual with crosscurrents of change and possibility intermingling across borders in the Middle East and elsewhere.

If the center of Jewish hope and prayer is demilitarized and divorced from the state, then the diaspora reality of Jewish history is reasserted. This diaspora is less a return implying that history can be reversed and the abuse of power within statehood can be dismissed, than it is a looking forward. The encounter between Jews and Palestinians and the solidarity that emerges from this encounter will be the focal point. Like the Jewish and Christian reconciliation in the West and its effects on Jewish and Christian religiosity, a static embrace is an attempt to freeze, ignore, or transcend the past to protect from the void and the future. As with Jews and Palestinians, so, too, with Jews and Christians in the West. It is not a question of whether each community has its own integrity, rights, and responsibilities—an obvious affirmation—but how the limits of each community will be diminished and the possibilities of each enhanced.

Religions, like states, divide and structure what is shared and moving. They make boundaries of that which has recently been crossed. They attempt to keep the new boundaries from being crossed. These are the boundaries that keep states militarized and with them the religions of their inhabitants. Only religions and spiritualities that seek to maintain boundaries and eliminate that which challenges them can be militarized by power and politics.

☙

IS THIS DIASPORA within the Holy Land Jewish? This question returns each time I land in Tel Aviv. I know that Israel, like any state, does not bring life. Only when structured for justice can it provide a framework that enhances life.

Atrocity diminishes the human capability to affirm God and each other. A diaspora cannot definitively counter what injustice bequeaths. It can only provide a psychological and geographic space to work through the questions and join with others in doubt and affirmation.

After leaving Auschwitz, I traveled to South Africa. There, the difficult transition from apartheid to democracy was taking place. Israel had been involved for many years in South Africa, often on the side of the apartheid regime, with armaments and advisors as in Latin America, but this time with more: a shared nuclear program spanning decades. Both countries practiced injustice. Both countries felt isolated. They developed nuclear weapons because they feared their surroundings.

The time to overturn apartheid had come. I listened with over one hundred thousand South Africans to the words of Nelson Mandela at the funeral of a revolutionary fighter, Chris Hani. Just days earlier Hani was gunned down at his home by a white supremacist, his daughter by his side. As in Latin America, the South African church had been split for many years. White supremacy had legitimated and been subverted by Christianity. Transitions are always difficult. The change in South Africa is monumental.

Could there be a reconciliation with justice in South Africa? The broken middle there, as elsewhere, is complicated. Still the Bantustans had no future. Nor did the white ghettos that once ruled over the Black and colored townships. Massive bloodshed and chaos hung in the air as a possibility, and the stadium crowd, impatient with the long struggle, clamored for an immediate change that would relieve them of the last vestiges of apartheid.

There is little question that Israel's links with South Africa were links with the Nazi past. The separation of peoples, racial classifications, and slave labor camps are reminders of the Nazi period. Even the "autonomy" within certain areas reminds one of the Nazis *and* what has evolved in the expansion of Israel. South African Blacks understood the situation of Palestinians for this reason. What they are now overcoming, Palestinians are still suffering.

Traveling the diaspora in the Third World and the Holy Land can only be complete, at least for a Jew, by traveling to Germany. Germany is different. Here it all began.

The trauma of the Holocaust remains an event that, despite all the historical explanations and analysis, is difficult for me to comprehend. In their utter depravity, the Nazis stretched the human limits of atrocity. The magnitude of destruction and death is one level, though Stalinism rivals the Nazis in this category. Perhaps it was the relentlessness of the pursuit of every living Jew and the desire to extinguish Jewish life from the world. The sense of conspiracy and biological invasion that Jews represented for the Nazis remains unique in its horror.

How did this madness became the norm? Are the Germans I meet infected by an anti-Jewish virus that, turned in a certain direction, issues in atrocity? Traveling through Germany is a reminder of this anti-Semitism. For a Jew of my generation, each raised voice and manner can be a reminder of the Nazi era only recently banished from the earth.

In Germany, the past is horrible to confront. The juxtaposition of the past and the present is difficult in a different way. Germany is a normal country as countries go. Life is carried on just as it is everywhere in the West. Germany's economic power in Europe is again dominant and the scars of war are only visible through the architecture from the 1950s and 1960s. Nearly the entire infrastructure of Germany was destroyed in the war and with it many of the memories that are carried by the structure of cities and the cultures that inform it. Germans born after the war and visitors who come to Germany today are thus released from some of the memories that could have invoked the horrors of the Nazi period. Those are reserved for the concentration and death camps like Dachau and Bergen-Belsen that lie on the outskirts of cities. They are tucked away.

I first traveled to Germany in 1986 at the invitation of the German theologian Dorothee Soelle. We met at a conference in New York where she delivered a lecture on Germany and the peace movement. The overall theme of the conference was the interrelationship of Marxism and Christianity as developed in theologies emanating from Latin America and Europe. I was asked to listen to the conference lectures and prepare a response that highlighted the interrelationship between them. As an outsider to Latin America, Europe, Christianity, and Marxism, I was asked to interpret those committed to certain positions and religions.

Soelle visited me one evening in my hotel room as I was preparing my response. As a Protestant Christian, Soelle is very much opposed to the nuclearization of Europe and warns against the possibility of nuclear war. Her reasons are obvious and the sources of her struggle clear. As a Christian, she cannot accept the threat or use of weapons of mass destruction. She opposes nuclear weapons for the death they would bring, but also in relation to the destruction her own people had caused during the Nazi period. Soelle's memory of that period is vivid because her childhood was lived within it. Her father was a resistor against the Nazi regime and was imprisoned. She sees her opposition to the nuclearization of Europe in continuity with that resistance.

We spoke well into the evening on these subjects. It was an emotional evening that flowed into the early morning hours. She asked if I had ever been to Germany and when I replied yes, but only as a student traveling without contacts, she invited me to her home in Hamburg. I was excited by this invitation because it would be a chance to travel and meet Germans in the context of their lives today. What do Germans think about the past? How do they view the present in light of the past?

My arrival in Hamburg coincided with two significant events. The first was personal, the pregnancy of my wife with our first son, Aaron. The second was global, with the disaster at the Chernobyl nuclear generating plant in the Soviet Union. Even weeks after that event the consequences of that disaster were only dimly outlined. They were also predictable. The contamination of the immediate area with death was assumed. Malformation and cancer for generations could be expected. The extension of the contamination through the atmosphere beyond the immediate borders of the Soviet Union was probable.

The campaign against nuclearization that Soelle supported draws strength through her politics and theology. She sees nuclear weapons as a concrete manifestation of a broader problem of technology and militarization used for profit and power. Structuring the wealthy countries along these lines means poverty for other countries. That is why her own organizing stretched from Germany to the United States and to Latin America. Soelle also was traveling the diaspora. Her relentless energy stood alongside her almost gaunt appearance. The Chernobyl disaster simply confirmed her point of view and increased her determination. It was almost as if time was running out. Mass destruction and death would appear a second time in her lifetime. The race against the nuclear clock was a race against a final victory of the Nazi era she had lived through. This time the destruction of Europe and the Jews would be extended to all of humanity.

My time with Soelle and her husband, Fulbert Steffensky, was important. Steffensky is also a theologian, a former Catholic monk, and a professor at Hamburg University. Unlike Soelle, he preferred to separate the Holocaust and the issue of nuclear weapons. Though one had accomplished mass death and the other held open the possibility of universal death, he worried that joining the two might allow the universal to absorb the particular. For Steffensky, the Holocaust stands alone.

Continuity is an important issue to both Soelle and Steffensky because the Holocaust divides German history and culture into a "before" and "after." The present generation searches for a bridge across this divide. For some, activism for a demilitarized Europe is that bridge. Going back is impossible, but how to move forward is a daunting challenge. Though he realizes that standing still is impossible, Steffensky is cautious about this movement ahead. Can a solidarity between the victims of the Holocaust and those who come from the culture that produced it lead to a solidarity in the present with all those who suffer and stand under the shadow of the nuclear menace?

During the same visit, I met three women from the peace organization Pax Christi who dedicated their lives to repentance for the Holocaust. One was Gisella Wiese. She was born just before Hitler came to power and lived through the Nazi era as a child. The other two, Marleis and Marei, were born after the Holocaust. The first Nazi trials that brought Jewish survivors back to testify in Germany were held in Frankfurt in the 1970s. These women arranged hospitality for the witnesses.

The witnesses had been brutally expelled from Germany and had lost family and friends to the murderous Nazis. Now they would face the perpetrators of those deeds. The reopening of wounds on the soil of their homeland was difficult enough. These three women sought to provide the simplest of comforts and accompaniment. They escorted witnesses to court, provided food and necessary items for their stay, talked and shared meals with them if they were alone.

Pax Christi is a Christian peace organization founded after World War II to promote peace in Europe. Their witness is derived from the gospel message of repentance and reconciliation, but, to my surprise, Christianity was rarely mentioned by the group. The horror of the Holocaust was front and center. We spent three days together without leaving the subject.

Their fear is the loss of memory. Modern Germany has come into its own and the new generation feels more and more distant from the Nazi era. The situation is complex because that which is distant is still near. The generational mixture of young and old, common to all societies, includes those who were alive and active during the Holocaust and those who were children or not yet born. Murderers walk the street with those who are innocent. Both walk in the shadow of brutality and death.

These women attempt to keep the memory of the Holocaust alive. They believe that forgetting the deeds of Germany in a new affluence consigns the victims of the Holocaust to oblivion. If Jews must remember the Holocaust, so, too, the Germans. The meaning of the Holocaust includes the victims *and* the perpetrators. The shadow of the Holocaust haunts both peoples.

Our discussions were deep and emotional. The women were unrelenting in their critique of German history. I came upon a problematic in German culture that almost defies solution. Germans can only reconcile their history in a forward movement. The population that Germans need to move forward with, German Jews, was eliminated from Germany as an integral and viable community. The welcoming of Jewish witnesses, as important and profound as it is, drives home the limitations of reconciliation. Without the continuation of Jews in German culture and life after the Holocaust, acts of repentance and mutual acceptance are abstracted from real life.

A substitute for an internal reconciliation is the payment of reparations and unquestioned support of Israel. Germans have toured Israel for years. They have worked on kibbutzim and affiliated with many mutual associations. However, they have identified with Jews at the expense of Palestinians, as if Israel is a Jewish drama without the involvement of others. Christians, including those from Pax Christi, have been especially active in solidarity with Israel.

Identifying with Jews is understandable and necessary. Can that solidarity be maintained when Germans recognize that the dream of Israel is a nightmare for Palestinians? Because solidarity with Jews is of necessity outside of Germany, a romantic image of Jews replaces the demonic image held by the Nazis. The question remains whether Germans can come into solidarity with Jews as a people in our suffering *and* in our abuse of power.

A romanticized image of a people is just a short step from a demonic image. Romantic images are destined to be sullied with reality. I realized in my conversations with the women from Pax Christi that "real" Jews would be difficult to discuss because they are absent from German culture and because reality is destined to disappoint. Jews symbolize the brokenness of German history. Jews promise rescue. If only enough money can be paid, enough solidarity shown, perhaps the demonic aspect of German history will fade. I wonder if it would return if Jews are recognized as a people with the same limitations and possibilities as Germans.

The demonic/romantic dichotomy of Jews in the German psyche mirrors the romantic/demonic dichotomy that many Jews have of themselves and Germans in relation to German history. Because of the honesty of these women, I heard for the first time the confession of German sins vis-à-vis my own people. I knew, however, that the story did not stop in the Nazi era. The Jewish culture they knew was murdered and should be mourned for its own sake. Anything that speaks to that lost culture—survivors, Yiddish, memorials—is to be honored. After three days of discussion of the Holocaust, I realized the need to recognize our own continuation as a people. We are alive in history and mourning has given way to a celebration of Jewish life. Equally important, though, is the mourning as a cover for injustice or celebration that continues at another's expense.

On the last day of our meeting, I began to speak of Israel as a response to the Holocaust and as a bridge in our own history. The bridge goes one way, from Auschwitz to Jerusalem, but the other side of the bridge, to the Palestinians and to others struggling for justice, has yet to be built. There is no path forward with the Germans in relation to Jews except in a romanticized way destined to disappoint. There is a path forward for Jews because Israel and Palestine are still interconnected on the land and in societal proximity.

An authentic solidarity with Jewish history can only be achieved by Germans if they also build a bridge to the Palestinian people. Of course, those Germans who come into solidarity with the Palestinian people, *as if Israel just appeared on the map without cause and without German responsibility,* fail to take responsibility for their own history. At the same time, uncritical support for Israel creates a myth about their own future. That myth is that the brokenness of German culture can be transcended without Jews. The broken middle of Germany in relation to Jews is solidarity with Jews *and* Palestinians. That is the only internal reckoning with the past and present possible for a Germany that seeks to deal honestly with its own concrete memory of atrocity.

The difficulties here are enormous. I have met Germans who can hold the two sides of this question together. They are rare. Something happened in Germany that broke history into a before and after. This break is different from the brokenness that has a middle because the break is so devastating. Still, life goes on. Though the way through the impasse is almost impossible to navigate, the need remains.

I continued to move on the question of Israel and Palestine. What I shared of my evolving understandings of the bridge of solidarity between the Jews and Palestinians with the women, my friends understood. They were also fearful. Jewish empowerment rescues them from the final consequences of Hitler's policies and from the finality of their own guilt. Israel is a sign of the survival of Jews and the triumph of the good. Germany has forgotten the evil, or seeks to, and its reunification adds to that process. Israel is a barrier to a German return to being anti-Jewish. If return to those policies is accomplished, Israel will protect Jews from their consequences.

In conversations with Germans over the years, I wonder whether Israel is primarily for Jews or as much for Germans. Does Israel protect Jews from those who hate the Jewish people or does it protect Germans from themselves? Surely Germans fear the power and proclivities of their own country. In relation to Israel their understandings are different. As for many Jews, Israel *has* to be different for Germans. Evidence that proves otherwise is ignored.

Perhaps this is why many of the theologians, including Dorothee Soelle, have difficulty commenting on Israel. Many stay away from Israel and spurn invitations to meet with Palestinians. They speak on every other issue of justice except this one.

Like the delegates at Auschwitz, they are stuck, and understandably so. But when is this inability to move the beginning of a second crime, first against the Jews, then against the Palestinians? When do their works of justice and mercy become suspect in that silence?

&

THE YEAR AFTER my travel to Auschwitz, I was again in Germany speaking to the women of Pax Christi. They greeted me with emotion, as our time together had been so important for all of us. For me it had been the first contact with Germans who repented fully and unequivocally. For them it was the arrival of another "survivor," part of the next generation of Jews after the attempt to eliminate us from the earth. They understood my need to speak out even though they could not. Our mutual respect deepened.

I listened to more Germans tell their haunting stories of Nazis in their family background and the terrible and intimate suspicion of their parents' role in the final solution. I met a middle-aged woman whose mother has a picture of Hitler kissing her older sister when she was a baby. Today it is framed and displayed as it was during the Nazi era—on the mantle of the fireplace. I met a young man whose grandparents were among the earliest supporters of Hitler. They remained supportive long after the war was over. When I asked what he thought of his recently deceased grandparents he was torn. On the one hand he unequivocally deplored their support of Hitler. On the other hand they were loving, even doting grandparents. I returned again to the past.

At this same moment, I was coming to the end of the era of Auschwitz. I was reeling from my trip to Auschwitz and the crushing of the first Palestinian uprising. As a people we are alive rather than dead. Our mourning of the dead leads to still more death. Even with the right intentions and for the right reasons, the dead are being used to insulate us from the living. The challenge lies beyond the mourning. It lies beyond Israel and Germany.

Should there be a call to end the mourning in Germany, or, as the Jewish theologian called for us to do at Auschwitz, to let the memory decay with time and nature? The women of Pax Christi are horrified at that thought. I understand why. Like Jews, they have grown used to the protection afforded them by this most gruesome memory.

To move forward means the possibility of return. In Germany the return cannot involve Jews since the community does not exist within. Prejudice exists for other minorities, Turkish people and Gypsies especially, who are often seen through the prism of the Jewish experience. How long will it take for Germans to see the minorities of today without the baggage of yesterday? If they deal with Germany today in and for itself, will they have to deal with Jews in the same way?

These questions are for another generation in Germany. My admiration for those who take their history seriously remains. The break in German history is so great that they can only observe the present from the past. That Jews are alive gives them great comfort, but for me that is only the beginning.

The women of Pax Christi fight for the past. The imperative is to fight for a future.

9

A Public Confession

AFTER TRAVELING TO AUSCHWITZ, I was asked to speak at Union Theological Seminary in New York City on the future of the Jewish life. James Cone, the founder of a Black theology of liberation and a professor at Union, extended the invitation. I had read Cone for many years and came to know him at Maryknoll. Over the years I invited him to lecture and teach summer courses at the institute I directed.

Cone is an enigma. In public life he is a powerful speaker and presence. In private he is shy and withdrawn. Cone was raised in Arkansas, part of the segregationist South where he developed a distance and anger toward whites and white power. He carries that distance even today.

Cone's early theology of Black power is filled with a justifiable rage and defiance. His vision of white Christianity is filled with demonic imagery. White Christianity is an evil that is to be overcome. It was a purveyor of the slave trade and slavery. Now it legitimizes segregation and racism. Only a Black Christianity can rescue African Americans from the demonic regime of white power in America. Whites can be rescued by identifying with a Christianity emanating from the struggle of African Americans to be free. Though Blacks are the principal victims of white power and Christianity today, others have suffered as well. In his early work, Cone includes Native Americans and Jews in this category.

Though Cone has lived his adult life in the North and in a seminary surrounding that is primarily white, his distance from whites remains. Over the years the almost exclusive identification of suffering and revolution with Blackness and the role of Black Christianity as a path forward has been criticized by others and has become less emphasized in his own writing. The theological world has become global in its reach, partly because of his writing, but in that globalization the particularity of the African American experience has receded. It is no longer possible to raise the banner of revolution in the name of one people, even though the special place of African Americans in the history of the United States is difficult to deny. The African diaspora in the Americas has become one among many diasporas. The voice of one must be the voice of all.

In his later work, Cone acknowledges this extension. Still, his passion remains with the particularity of the Black experience. His experience is somewhat like those suffered by the Latin American liberationists: his language has been absorbed, to some extent taken seriously, and co-opted as well. The "universality" of Christianity has won. Cone's work is a footnote within its larger framework.

In *Black Power and Black Theology,* published in 1969, Cone struggled with two figures who had then been recently murdered, Martin Luther King Jr. and Malcolm X. King's Christianity made sense to Cone then only in relation to the Black Power that Malcolm, with others in the Black Power movement, represented. By 1970, in *A Black Theology of Liberation,* Cone's concern had already turned to the white memorialization of King as a way of depriving King of his deeply committed and specifically African American voice. Cone knew that the co-opting of King by white Christianity would be used to distance the more radical, non-Christian voice of Malcolm X.

Little did he realize that both voices could be blended into a harmonious whole and that millions of white Americans would view movies of both men as if their messages spoke to them of peace and harmony in a divided world. Perhaps Cone's major work, *Martin and Malcolm and America,* published in 1992, is part of this harmonization. He sees both figures now as part of a broader affirmation of Christian failing, repentance, and hope. Cone's conclusion is that both voices are needed. This is especially true of the later King who protested the Vietnam war and developed a more critical view of American democracy, and the later Malcolm, who saw the need for diverse groups to come together in the struggle for justice and an integrated and diverse religiosity.

I started reading *Martin and Malcolm and America* on the plane to Poland. My reaction to the book was mixed. The book had taken Cone years to write. I could hear the cadence of his voice in the words on the page. I felt that part of Cone was in this book. Yet I also felt that part of his had been left behind. The world Cone lives in today, with his personal success and with the broader access African Americans have to American society, affects his writing. The constant demand to broaden his vision to include others is also part of the change. Still further is his own recognition that the position of African Americans in American society has changed and that those elements of empowerment found within his community and church are prone to the same temptations of others who have oppressed them.

The crosscurrents of traveling and living the diaspora force reappraisals and unexpected diversions. Perhaps Cone realizes what I am coming to understand within my own tradition; that all traditions and communities are limited and that empowerment changes the focus and potentialities of both. Yet this hardly diminishes the continuing problematic facing African Americans. For while Cone has achieved a starlike status in the world of academic theology, his life outside the academy can revert quickly to the status that many African Americans experience in the United States.

As I paused in my reading and looked around at the passengers on the plane, I reflected that traveling and writing is different from living the diaspora. In living the diaspora, the everyday confronts people in their different identities and calls forth a more immediate, sometimes gut-wrenching response. As a Jew or an African American, for example, the basis for speaking out is often scripted by the audience, and with time that external script becomes internalized. The give-and-take of a public life is complicated by these scripts. Only through self-discipline and reflection does the public figure continue on with integrity.

Cone's invitation to speak at Union provoked reflection on several levels. It was unusual for him to sponsor someone white. He did so as a sign of solidarity for my evolving views on the challenges before the Jewish people. It also brought me back to similarities and differences of Jewish and African American history.

So much has been written about the Jewish-Black alliance from the civil rights days and how that alliance has frayed over the debates on affirmative action and Israel. Though Cone has never written about these aspects of history and contemporary life, he is quite aware of the emotions surrounding these debates. He understands my position that in America the color line is the divide rather than the division between Jew and Christian. He also understands my view that in our empowerment, Jewish leadership has chosen to identify with white power rather than the African American struggle. Jews and African Americans who understand this situation may be a bridge beyond the leadership in both communities. They may begin to travel the diaspora in a more honest way.

As with many liberal Protestant seminaries, Union has been attentive to the Jewish struggle and the need for ecumenical partnership in the post-Holocaust age. Across the street from Union is Jewish Theological Seminary, the training ground for rabbis in the conservative tradition. The cooperation between Union and Jewish Theological is a close one.

This is part of a tradition of cooperation stretching back to such legendary figures as Reinhold Niebuhr at Union and Abraham Joshua Heschel at Jewish Theological. These two men helped establish the legitimacy of the ecumenical dialogue at the very heart of American religious and political culture. Both were public advocates of the inclusion of African Americans and Jews into the mainstream of American life. Both strongly supported Israel. They were so close that Heschel played a central role in Niebuhr's memorial service and delivered the final benediction at the grave site.

By the 1990s, that cooperation had turned into a deal. Union, a progressive, even radical, Christian seminary, announced the need to liberate those who struggle around the world. It is strangely silent on the issue regarding Jews and Palestinians. It is understood that this is a Jewish issue to be handled by Jewish Theological, though that institution is silent as well. The curriculum of Jewish Theological is oriented to biblical and rabbinic studies, with a smattering of courses in Jewish history. In relation to the formation and expansion of Israel, little is taught or said.

Trained in the texts of the traditions and the ability to guide congregations largely ignorant of those texts, Jewish seminary students are a bridge between the Jewish tradition and their congregants who are busy pursuing life in a Christian and secular America. In public, outside of the synagogue, the new rabbis, like many of the more experienced ones, act simply to deflect critical public discussion on Israel. They enforce a silence on Christians who want to speak publicly.

Dissenting Jews are also silenced. Since critical discussion on the central issues facing Jews is largely absent in the core curriculum of the seminary, how could one expect rabbis to speak intelligently on these issues? Protection rather than critical engagement becomes the *modus vivendi* of the rabbinic establishment.

Over the years of the ecumenical dialogue/deal, respect for the authenticity of Jewish life and the right of Jews to define themselves has, in many cases, evolved into simple Christian cowardice. The Jewish establishment, including the Anti-Defamation League, is hard on those who step out of line on the issue of Israel. The rabbis appeal to the spirit of ecumenical relations. At least to their minds, an honest dialogue might revive anti-Jewish stereotypes. Do Christians want to be responsible for that?

Another issue is how Jews function for Christians in the West. After demonizing Jews for centuries, Christian theology rediscovered the beauty of the Jewish tradition, especially in the Hebrew Bible. The Hebrew prophets play a strong role in Christian renewal, as does repentance for the Holocaust. The prophets help place a static Jesus in motion and free Christianity from an overemphasis on ritual and dogma. The Holocaust is a place of confession where the sins of Christianity are affirmed and, in that affirmation, cleansed. A paradox results. Jewish texts, traditionally seen as anticipating the messiah whom the Jewish community ultimately rejects, and Jewish victims, persecuted unto death by the religion that accepts the messiah "the Jews" rejected, become the vehicles for Christian renewal after the Holocaust.

The demonized Jew replaces the romanticized Jew, but unlike in Germany, where there is no sizable Jewish community, American Christians often interact with a sizable and empowered contemporary Jewish community. To keep a romanticized view means interacting under controlled circumstances with certain Jewish elites. Entire areas of discourse are off-limits.

The Jewish need for Christian support is obvious because of the cultural configuration of the West and its history. The politics of the integration of Jews into mainstream American culture, as well as the support of United States domestic and foreign policy for Jews and Israel, are clear. The need for a romanticized image of Jews for Christian identity and renewal is rarely discussed. Perhaps that is why Christians respond so easily to Jewish pressure. Would the realization that Jews are neither to be demonized nor romanticized force a re-evaluation of Christian identity and renewal? Can the return to the sources of Christianity, a return often as romanticized and manipulated by Christian forces for renewal as by their counterparts in Jewish renewal, be jeopardized by interacting with the reality of Jewish life?

Cone is outside this particular deal because African Americans adopted the Hebrew scriptures in their struggle against the Christianity of the slaveholders. As slaves in America they identified with the Hebrew slaves in Egypt. African Americans are drawn to the Exodus and the prophets because they see their own story in these events and personages. The need is for empowerment rather than renewal. African Americans encounter Jews in the political arena and in the narrative of suffering rather than in ecumenical conferences.

Since the Jewish establishment wants to identify with the Christian power that matters politically, white Christians are the target population. The Christianity that African Americans practice is inconsequential in this regard and so it is neglected by the Jewish establishment. Cone is certainly aware of the power of the Jewish establishment to brand anti-Jewish anyone who thinks critically about Jewish and Israeli policies.

Cone could ignore the warning issued by the Jewish establishment in its attack on Jesse Jackson during his bid for the presidency in 1988. Jackson reportedly made a derogatory comment about Jews in private *and* also had made positive comments about Yassir Arafat and the Palestine Liberation Organization in public. The uproar over Jackson's private and public speech was immediate. He was made to pay an incredible price. No doubt Cone remembers how United Nations Ambassador Andrew Young had been forced to resign his position in 1978 because he met in secret with representatives of the PLO. Once branded, the anti-Semite label rarely can be erased. Cone steers clear of a minefield that few have crossed without disaster.

Still, the invitation was extended and I accepted. While checking my calendar, a complication arose unbeknownst to the secretary who arranged the date for my lecture. The month was October and the date I agreed to was Yom Kippur, the holiest and most solemn day of the Jewish calendar. Yom Kippur comes at the end of a period of reflection ushered in by the Jewish New Year and is the day when, according to tradition, the books are sealed and God judges our lives as they have been and will be. Reflection gives way to confession, and, on Yom Kippur, Jews ask forgiveness for sins. As in the tradition of mourning, ritual has the dual function of allowing human beings to face each other and to face God.

Yom Kippur is important in other ways as well. When I was growing up in the 1950s and 1960s, this holy day became a symbol of Jewish authenticity and recognition from the larger society of Judaism as a respected religion in America. Few of my generation forget the importance of the ace left-handed pitcher, Sandy Koufax, refusing to pitch in a World Series game because of Yom Kippur. What this day actually means to Jews religiously is of less importance than what it stands for politically and socially. When Yom Kippur was received by the country as an important holiday it was a sign of the mainstreaming of Jews in America.

When I realized the significance of the date, I hesitated. I had to decide if I would speak on that date and I had to alert Union that it was Yom Kippur. At one level, the Jewish holy day should have no significance for a lecture at a Christian seminary. But with Jewish Theological across the street, I knew the possible ramifications for the school. With their knowledge, we agreed to the lecture for that date.

On Yom Kippur, Jews disappear into synagogues and homes. Our absence is a public affirmation of Jewishness. Yet on the day of personal and communal confession, what in fact occurs? Do we focus on personal transgressions and the public affirmation of our Jewishness? Or do we focus as well on the public policies of our community?

Since this is a day when significantly more Jews attend synagogue than usual, the rabbis use their sermons to speak of the need to affirm Jewishness and Jewish unity. Little is said about the corporate nature of Jewish life and, if spoken about, it is in the context of the need for active participation. Issues that concern Jews over the years are discussed. These include support for Israel, the campaign to free Soviet Jewry, and warnings about assimilation. The need to look critically at Israel is rarely mentioned.

If Palestinians are mentioned at all on Yom Kippur it is in the framework of terrorism. When the Oslo accords were signed just weeks before Yom Kippur and Rabin shook Arafat's hand, the rabbis were quite nervous about their sermon preparations. Yom Kippur sermons often demonized the Palestinians and now the Jewish community, including first and foremost the rabbis, had to be re-educated.

As a people, we have never confessed to the Palestinians on Yom Kippur or any other day of the year. In the synagogues, the rabbis are silent. Those who want to voice this confession on the day of atonement are not invited to speak. Even if allowed to speak in the synagogue, however, is that enough? By speaking to Jews we confess to ourselves and to God, but the tradition is that you first go to those you have wronged. A confession among Jews, a significant start to be sure, is not enough. The confession has to be public, outside of the synagogue, where all can hear, including Palestinians.

That is how I thought of my lecture that evening at Union. From the perspective of the Jewish community, it was a violation of the Jewishness we embrace in America. It was a statement that I had to make. The Yom Kippur liturgy is beautiful and haunting. It no longer fulfills the demands of confession. It has become a place of hiding rather than confrontation, a place of safety rather than of risk. Like Christianity, at least the Christianity of the affluent, the result is known in advance. God forgives and restores our innocence. Injustice continues.

ـ&

As I ARRIVED for my lecture I looked across from Union to Jewish Theological. It was virtually empty. The rabbinic students had flown to smaller synagogues around the country to officiate at these solemn services. The content of the sermons was predictable. Few of these future leaders of the Jewish community would risk themselves in speaking the confession that resides at the heart of Jewish life. The young and eager men and women who are dedicating their lives to serve the Jewish community would not serve by leading in the most painful of areas sanctioned by the Jewish calendar.

Yom Kippur is the day of fasting and hard questions. Jews are commanded to face themselves and others. If not Palestinians, could they at least speak of assimilation less in terms of intermarriage than in our assimilation to power and the state? If this were discussed, how long could the Palestinian question be denied? The young rabbis can hardly be faulted if their teachers and the rabbis they intern with are also silent.

As I began my lecture, I thought back on my time at Auschwitz. One of the professors at Jewish Theological, David Roskies, had been part of the delegation. Like me, he arrived early to visit Warsaw. I was glad to meet him because I had read his work on the Holocaust and the witness of Jewish artists, poets, and writers during that time. Their sensibilities had been severely tested in the ghettoization and destruction of the communities they lived in. Roskies showed how they reverted to the archetypes of Jewish history, especially to the Jewish liturgy of destruction. This liturgy had developed over time and had become a way for Jews to see their present destruction in a larger and more meaningful pattern. The Temple had been destroyed and Jews lived on. It was similarly true of the various inquisitions and pogroms throughout Jewish history.

These archetypes helped Jews remember those who committed violence against us. They also helped us remember our own dead. In its constant recitation in religious liturgy, these archetypes spread throughout the Jewish world and became part of our consciousness. Then memory became an avenue of expressing our woes in the present and even in death triumphing over our enemies. That is why artists in the Warsaw ghetto reflected on their situation in terms of the destruction of the Temple and the Spanish Inquisition. And that is why a Jewish poet spent his last days before deportation translating the Psalms into Yiddish. When he arrived for deportation, he dressed in prayer shawl and teffilin.

Roskies' work affected me in a powerful way. To be in Warsaw together with him was special. We traveled to the Jewish cemetery of Warsaw where many of the people he had written about were buried. We also went to the museum that had the milk canisters in which Emmanuel Ringelblum buried his diaries of his days in the ghetto. These diaries amount to a history of the ghetto. They were discovered beneath the rubble of Warsaw after the war.

Roskies was clearly moved, as was I. He also was angry with me. A few years before my travel to Auschwitz, I wrote of Roskies' liturgy of destruction in light of the present. I suggested that the Jewish memory of destruction had broadened with the founding of Israel. It now needed to include the Palestinian people. At the outset, this broadening might seem theoretical, something that would happen in the future, but in my research I found that Jews had already recognized that broadening. I read reports of Jewish soldiers who, in the 1948 war, refused to kill unarmed Palestinians civilians because Jewish civilians had been murdered throughout history. I read reports of other soldiers who, in witnessing the mass deportation of Palestinians from their homes and land, saw them as Jews who had been exiled from the land when the Temple was destroyed.

Seeing the Palestinians in terms of Jewish history is obvious. How else can we see the history of another people except through our own particular journey? What is important here, however, is the intuitive sense that what was happening to Palestinians had happened to us. Where once others were culpable, now we are culpable.

The liturgy of destruction has become inclusive of Palestinians because Jews have seen it expand before us and at our hands. Rather than discovering this inclusive liturgy of destruction, what amazes me is how we have repressed it, *as if the suffering of Palestinians at our hands can be repressed forever and the liturgies of our synagogues and the work of our artists can survive this violation of another people without change.*

Roskies had heard of my work. After visiting the museum and standing before Ringelblum's canisters, he told me he was offended by my use of the liturgy of destruction. It was a strange moment. We were standing before a witness to the Holocaust who is remembered precisely because he wrote a history of his time without flinching and without embellishment. This included scathing denunciations of Jewish leadership. In his diaries, Ringelblum details the terror of the Nazis, the struggle for survival by Jews, and the failings of Jews themselves. Ringelblum, as a Jew and a historian, let the chips fall where they may. It was a sign of fidelity to Jews and to the world.

The transposition of Ringelblum and Roskies mirrors the transposition of Jewish history. Ringelblum was ghettoized and destined for death. He wrote the truth. Roskies is affluent and tenured. He writes of the honesty of Ringelblum and deflects the most obvious of questions suggested by his work. Ringelblum recorded the present. Roskies evokes only the past.

As I looked out at the audience at Union, filled with feminists, African Americans, gays and lesbians, Asians and Africans, and those white Europeans and Americans who sought to bring their history to a critical consciousness, I realized I had crossed the final boundary.

Across the room was James Cone. The Yom Kippur liturgy was beginning in synagogues across the country. I had little choice but to make this confession. This was the only liturgy I could participate in with integrity.

On Yom Kippur the message was clear. My confession had become my prayer.

ૐ

WHEN I LEFT UNION that night, I felt the lecture had gone well. Yet I was overcome by a sense of emptiness. I felt an acute sense of aloneness.

After the lecture I was invited by a group of professors to a reception. Cone excused himself. He was flying out early in the morning to give lectures in the Midwest.

The informal discussion at the reception revolved around Yom Kippur. A Catholic liturgist on the faculty at Union questioned whether violating a public taboo on this holy day would help the Jewish community hear the issues I was raising. She wondered whether it would encourage the opposite, the violation becoming an excuse not to listen. She was close to some of the faculty at Jewish Theological and knew that this would be their response.

I asked her to advise me how I could be faithful in this situation. It surprised me when she counseled participation in an internal Jewish discussion when she, as Catholic liturgist and religious sister, spent her working days at a Protestant seminary. Conducting public liturgies is denied her in the Catholic community. Teaching at a Protestant seminary was a way of declaring her right and ability to be a full and equal leader in religious life.

She understood the contradiction in her own life but, in her mind, the Jewish situation was different. The blending of Protestant and Catholic into a transformed and unified Christianity is a goal to be treasured. The schism between the two churches was unfortunate in its origin. The strengths of both traditions can be brought back together now, hopefully without their limitations. Jews remain distinct, outside of these traditions. I wondered: Is Judaism foreign to Christianity historically? Have Judaism and Jews lived on another planet for the past two thousand years?

For some reason it is impossible for Judaism to be reunited with the traditions to which it gave birth and to benefit from their strengths and jettison some of their limitations. Jewish texts and spiritualities are found within Christianity by Christians, a reality the Catholic liturgist was more than ready to affirm. The idea that Jews can find in Christianity part of themselves, and that Christianity can also contribute its own themes to Jews and Judaism, is more difficult to acknowledge.

A broader tradition of faith and struggle can be affirmed by Christians as part of their own journey. That same broader tradition cannot be embraced by Jews without abandoning their special place for Christians in religious history and eschatology. Jewish leadership concurs with this proposition. Enlarging the terrain of embrace is to become something other than Jewish rather than recognizing that the historical breaks with these communities can be gathered together in a different synthesis.

Were not each of these communities and traditions formed by people who came from somewhere else into a new understanding of God and justice? Abraham was not Jewish. Nor were the tribes that formed the Israelite nation. Jesus and his disciples were neither Catholic nor Protestant. Martin Luther was a dissenting Catholic.

All over the world I meet those who are crossing in and out of different traditions. They are enlarging the terrain of their embrace. Most are recovering aspects of their traditions that have been torn away by colonialism or by atrocity. Some embrace elements of indigenous life discarded through violence and colonialism. They recover aspects of culture and religiosity that would have been unthinkable in previous generations.

As I traveled the diaspora, I witnessed this happening in Christianity throughout the world. After a decade of such travel, I decided that Christianity, as it exists in the world—in practice—is so diverse as to be undefinable. We live in a world that experiences so much boundary crossing that any assumed purity is a denial rather than an affirmation of reality. All cultures have experienced colonialism and religious proselytization. They are experiencing it today, if not overtly from traditional religions, then certainly in the guise of modernity. What power does Christianity or Judaism, Islam or Hinduism, have in the face of the onslaught of modernity? Today modernity is the major force of colonialism and evangelization. Perhaps modernity is the major religion of our time. To this power all bow.

The Catholic sister at a Protestant seminary is one attempt to benefit from and find a way through modernity. When Catholicism and Protestantism are defining in their own integrity and power, it is unthinkable for Catholics and Protestants to forge a spirituality together. The dilution of their power allows this alliance. Modernity demands it. People of faith are at the crossroads of their sensibility and their history. *Only by joining forces in a critical understanding of our times can people of faith and commitment continue to evolve and deepen.*

Ecumenical relations and dialogue were the first steps toward this new synthesis. Yet to remain in that modality today is to continue what is now behind us. It is to spend our time renewing our traditions and making peace within them, as if the world is whole and just, as if these traditions, separated and paraded in updated liturgies and modern sensibilities, address the times in which we live.

Why have I found so many others traveling the diaspora with me, often speaking of their renewed particularities to appreciating audiences of different particularities? Why do the people speaking of this beauty do so before others if not to understand their search better than the particularities from which they came? At some point the particularity has to be seen within a commonality that is forming in the renewal itself.

I often feel that those who speak of renewal should admit what other conservative proponents of particularity charge: they have arrived somewhere other than where they began. The insistence on finding the true faith, whether in Jewish renewal or Christian liberation theology, belies the evolution the representatives themselves embody.

Traveling the diaspora brings this question home. Neither the conservatives nor the progressives represent "true" Judaism or Christianity. "True" religion does not exist historically or in the present. The definition of a particular religion or identity found within that religion is an attempt to provide meaning by creating and structuring a reality. The definition itself, though, gives birth to an identity through which we can define ourselves. Grounding ourselves in these definitions and ritualizing them does what Viktor Frankl and

Lawrence Langer argued over in relation to the Holocaust—that is, the creation of meaning where none is self-evident.

Once grounded, these definitions take on a life of their own. Typically we anchor these definitions and identities in an ontological reality. Through this we seek to protect ourselves from the next threat to meaning and purpose. Christianity has a long history of destroying the definitions and ontologies of others and defending its own once in power. Jewish definitions and identities barely survive annihilation and then assert them as a power over another people. Even those being persecuted by these definitions and identities often hold on to them as if they carry an intrinsic meaning. Is this why the liberation theologians I meet argue for the center of the Christian tradition even as it is being used against them and their people? Perhaps this is why those in Jewish renewal fight for the center as well, even though the force of their argument is also part of the displacement of the Palestinian people.

Unable to admit the end, the future is being created without acknowledgment. Hence the emptiness I felt as I left Union that night. Yom Kippur has evolved in Jewish history as a day of confession and now is a day where Jews disappear—only for a day—from the lives they lead. The rest of the year, Jews, like people of other religions, are involved in all sorts of activities that contradict the intention of that day and deflect from its fulfillment.

Perhaps the importance of confessional holidays is to sanction an everyday life in contradiction to its message. But where does that leave us? Jews attend Yom Kippur services where the central question facing us as a people becomes invisible. That invisibility is sanctioned by religious ritual. Confession becomes a way to avert our eyes.

For those who can no longer avert their eyes, what religion and ritual is left for them? If they do not seek another religion and ritual, as if they could in this way avoid the fate of the religions they come from, where do those who travel the diaspora turn? Their particularities have come to a dead end. Does the argument for its core realization simply prolong the agony and destination that is clear?

The secular option is fraught with many of the same difficulties. Here, a pretense of innocence and a civil war over the "core" values of the Enlightenment and modernity and their "correct" interpretation escalates. The battles between the advocates of democracy in its capitalist or socialist forms, between dealing with authoritarian regimes or standing firm for human rights, are like the arguments between conservative and renewal forces in religion. They beg the question of the cycle of violence and atrocity found within modernity. It is as if the way out is through discovery of an ontological anchor of secularity, defining identity and particularity as static realities.

Traveling the diaspora brings these arguments into focus. Like religion, I experience secularity as a failed system. When argued apart from its origins and the circumstances it exists within today, secularity becomes an abstraction. Secular life is floundering. Its rituals are also ways of averting the eyes. Is that why traditional religion is often used to shore up this aversion?

Looking back over the years, I have used Judaism and Christianity as well. At first I was reluctant. I identified with religious people but was wary of their language. In my college years I came into contact with the major religious figures and movements of our time. My teachers studied with Reinhold Niebuhr and Paul Tillich. As an undergraduate I heard Abraham Joshua Heschel speak and listened to him in a small group after his lecture. I read John Courtney Murray and was introduced to the life of Simone Weil. In my last year of studies I met Dorothy Day and spent an afternoon with Daniel Berrigan. I was fascinated by these giants of religious thought. I identified with their commitment. This helped me bridge their diverse faiths and languages.

Still, it was difficult for me to mouth these words of faith or affirm the God that they seemed to find so easily. I was torn even then between the God they affirmed and the God who was questioned in the Holocaust. Richard Rubenstein found in the Holocaust the end of traditional faith. Here I was confronted by those who affirmed faith despite and perhaps even because of the Holocaust. Rubenstein's ending was their beginning. The bridge that they found fascinated and eluded me at the same time. And yet I knew that the end that Rubenstein articulated was not enough.

Traveling the diaspora is a continuation of that search. I embody this tension between the end that Rubenstein foretold and the faith that Heschel, Day, and Berrigan held. Is there something that incorporates Rubenstein's end and Heschel's affirmation for the generation after the Holocaust? Can I say "no" as Rubenstein has to a God who allows the destruction of millions of Jews and "yes" to the affirmation of life as Day lived it in community among the poor? Can I listen and affirm both the liturgical cadences of Rubenstein *and* Berrigan, two who ostensibly stand at the opposite sides of faith and politics?

These tensions informed the next generation of theologians—the voices of Rosemary Radford Ruether, the great Catholic feminist theologian, of James Cone and Gustavo Gutiérrez, and so many others. They pose a diverse religious and political landscape that I am part of and can deny only by being dishonest. My own particular tradition, Judaism, like their particular traditions, can embrace these voices without becoming something other than its defining nature. The evolution is inside *and* out, so that a new configuration is necessary, a new language and ritual, and more. We need a freedom to embrace the voices that become part of one's life when traveling and living the diaspora. This may have been what Rubenstein meant when in later years he described me as representing the mainstream of neither Jewish nor Christian life.

I STILL FALL INTO A PATTERN of using both religions to shore up the thought and commitment I find important. Judaism is to be reclaimed as Christians are reclaiming Christianity, hence the need for a Jewish theology of liberation, a subject I explored in the 1980s. This theology hoped to speak to the essence of Judaism—the ethical core—and, in combination with a renewed Christianity, might bring forth a new age of ecumenical fraternity. The lessons of the Holocaust are heard and heeded. A Palestinian state emerges alongside Israel. The dynamic of Jewish life reasserts itself.

In Jerusalem in 1987, just months before the first Palestinian uprising, I broached these ideas in a public lecture at the Shalom Hartman Institute. I also included the need for confession and reparations to the Palestinian people. The room seated about eighty people comfortably. To my surprise almost two hundred people squeezed into this small area. The seats were full, others stood. The mood was electric.

The response was beyond anything I expected. Emotion was high. Michael Walzer, the well-known Jewish ethicist, responded to my talk. He condemned me and the ideas I spoke about in no uncertain terms. His anger could hardly be contained. As he spoke, his hands shook almost uncontrollably. At first I thought he had a medical condition, perhaps Parkinson's. I knew it could not be nervousness as Walzer was my senior in age and experience. Ultimately, I realized it was pure anger.

Walzer is a liberal. He had just published a book on how the Exodus story has been used by movements for justice throughout history. Like Roskies' objection to my use of his liturgy of destruction to include the Palestinians, Walzer objected to my use of liberation themes to include Jews and Palestinians together. When I spoke of the suffering in the Middle East and elsewhere, he identified himself in that category. As I listened to him, I wondered if a professor with lifetime tenure at the Institute for Advanced Studies at Princeton University really believes that when the poor are invoked he is among them.

David Hartman, the liberal and influential rabbi who founded and directs the institute, also attended my lecture and listened attentively to the comments by the respondents. Father Elias Chacour, a Palestinian and an Orthodox priest, responded after Walzer and related the story of his family's dispossession in the 1948 war and how difficult it is for Palestinians to live with dignity within the 1967 borders of Israel. Chacour is also a citizen of Israel. In his fight for justice he calls upon his Christian faith, his belonging to the larger Palestinian people, and his Israeli citizenship.

Always forceful and polite, Chacour's response countered Walzer's emotional presentation. During the first break of what would become a four-hour marathon session, Hartman approached Chacour and told Chacour that he had offended him. Chacour politely apologized for any offense and inquired what he had done to offend Hartman. "Your presence offends me," Hartman replied quickly.

Standing alone with people coming and going during the break and observing this encounter I felt a tremendous emptiness, not unlike the one I experienced later at Union. The audiences were different and the time was different as well, before *and* after the first Palestinian uprising. The emptiness had a different note to it. In Jerusalem I felt something leave me. Was it a hope I was holding onto? At Union I felt as if hope would have to come from within.

Perhaps hope is the wrong word. Rather a strength to continue my travels and living within the diaspora. Did my real experience in Jerusalem give birth the following year to my Jerusalem dream?

A tension surfaced between my call for Jewish accountability and the fact that even progressive Jewish voices were caught in a cycle they would not end. When the very presence of Palestinians is offensive, then the dream of Zion is a nightmare. The dreams of Jews within that nightmare can only reflect that sensibility and, in my case, the dream is one of diaspora *and* exile. I, with other Jews, will find my way among others, until a new path is found. Whether that way will be identifiably Jewish or not is open to question. Still the warnings are clear. The language of Jewish tradition cannot make this transition. Those like myself who attempt this are doomed to failure.

If the case of Judaism and contemporary Jewish life can no longer be argued with integrity, neither can the case of Christianity and Christian life. The Catholic sister at Union is only delaying the most obvious of questions or, through liturgical beauty, averting her eyes to the toll that atrocity has taken on Christianity. I can see the end of Jewish history in the abuse of the Palestinian people. This pales before the historic propensity of Christianity toward mass death and genocide. How can Christians continue to call out for justice in the name of their religion?

As Jews legitimate the ghettoization of Palestinians, I read the daily reports of Christians butchering each other in Rwanda. Between 500,000 and 700,000 Rwandans were killed within several months, a daily murder rate that surpassed the Nazis. I saw film footage of Orthodox priests in Bosnia blessing the cleansing of Muslims from their midst. Not that Islam is innocent in this cycle of violence and atrocity. In the 1990s, the slaughter in Algeria in the name of Islam testifies to this culpability. The Ramadan season was specially selected for an increase in terror. The reports of mass killings captured the headlines.

Atrocity, complicity, hypocrisy—is there no end to it? Since I was a young child I have been drawn to religiosity. In my adult years I have tried to explore and name a religiosity I can affirm. A battle ensues between the desire to embrace religiosity and the fear of embracing a religiosity untrue to the deepest impulses within me. The only religious language available to me is of the traditions I inherit, intimately Judaism, culturally Christianity. These languages are available *and* are so compromised. The ability to be understood by others and to understand myself is at issue. Perhaps this is why I, with others, fall back into traditional religious language, pushing away other experiences that might lead to another language.

My confrontation in Jerusalem, as did later the experience of the delegation at Auschwitz and my confession on Yom Kippur, speaks to these issues. So, too, the Jerusalem dream. Was the confrontation in Jerusalem also a nightmare? And why, at the end of the dream, when I awoke suddenly, having just survived certain death, did I feel at peace?

The Jerusalem dream was a nightmare. Or perhaps the nightmarish reality of Jerusalem, with Israeli soldiers beating Palestinian teenagers, bequeaths a dream where a way of fidelity is born. There is a choice, the dream tells me, in the diaspora *and* in the exile. This diaspora is found in the exile. The exile is found in the diaspora.

The dream/nightmare pointed the way to fidelity. Its discovery lay ahead.

10
God of Life

WHEN I ARRIVED IN COSTA RICA in May, 1988, it was warm and the hospitality of the Christians who invited me made me feel welcome. The group calls itself DEI, short for Deparamento Écumenico Investigaciones. They had just translated and published my book on a Jewish theology of liberation. The invitation was to publicly present my book and address their institute. To have my work translated into Spanish was special. I flew to Costa Rica anticipating a celebration.

It was also a serious trip. DEI sponsors programs on development, education, and grassroots organizing. The groups I addressed were filled with people working at the grassroots of their countries from Central and South America. Their work is important and sometimes dangerous. Some in the group had been tortured or would be one day. Some had lost friends in the struggle. Some might lose their own lives.

I felt strange as I addressed the various assemblies of activists. I come from a people who has suffered and is now empowered. I spoke to people who could only dream of the perils of empowerment. Their suffering was increasing.

One of the leaders of the group was Pablo Richard. I had met Richard at Maryknoll several years earlier. He was interested in continuing our discussions and we spent several Shabbats at my home in New York. Richard is a deeply intelligent and affable Chilean. His sense of humor can hide a difficult past. The reason he lives in Costa Rica is that he was exiled from Chile after the overthrow of democracy.

In our discussions it became clear to me that Richard is keenly aware of the historic suffering of the Jews. He sees the major heresy of historic Christianity flowing from its being anti-Jewish. This turning away from Jews ushered in the Constantinian era and the birth of Christendom.

Richard asked the local rabbi to co-host me and perhaps respond to my thinking on a Jewish liberation theology. The rabbi refused him and, knowing DEI's stance for the revolutionary government of Nicaragua, proffered his support of Ronald Reagan's funding of the Contras in Nicaragua. The rabbi, a son of a family exiled from Europe during the Nazi era, is himself Chilean. On Shabbat I decided to attend synagogue. The rabbi was there and he greeted me in a distant way and told me that he supported Augusto Pinochet, the dictator who overthrew the democratically elected government of Salvador Allende. Like the former Nicaraguan dictator, Pinochet was responsible for much violence and death. Pablo Richard was exiled by him. He barely escaped alive.

I was hardly surprised by such a rabbi. But I was surprised when I met the head of the publishing arm of this Christian liberation center, Jorge David Aruj. Aruj is a Jew from Argentina who had fought the dictatorship there. He was captured, tortured, and finally escaped.

Aruj was intrigued by my work. What intrigued him was not the struggle for liberation, for he had fought and suffered for that already. Nor was it the possibility that theology could support such a struggle. After all, he directed a publishing house that was explicitly doing just that. What intrigued him is the possibility that a Jewish theology can support such a struggle, that Judaism can actually lend a deeper meaning to what he was drawn to in the political realm.

In Argentina, Aruj had only been in contact with that part of the Jewish religious community that mirrored the judgments of the rabbi in Costa Rica. They were either silent in the face of oppression or in complicity with the generals. Like Richard, this Jewish publisher of Christian liberation theology had to flee for his life in the face of dictatorships too often supported by the religious establishments of both communities.

All of this served as a backdrop to my introduction of a Jewish theology of liberation to those who worked for liberation in almost impossible circumstances. What was I to say? How could I connect the experience of Jews with their experience? Speaking of the Holocaust in front of people who experience suffering in the here and now is more of a challenge than lecturing in a university or pointing out the flaws of biblical exegesis in theology. Those who struggle in the present humble discussion of past events.

I began my first talk with an obvious statement: as Jews and Christians we come from different traditions. Then, as I looked out over the faces of the people, I offered a second, less obvious statement: though from different traditions, our historical experience unites us. I then expanded on this second statement. The difference is usually and easily summed up in belief or disbelief in the messiah Jesus. Here Christians and Jews part company. Yet if we concentrate on the experience of peoples, we are joined. For the past centuries Latin Americans experienced a form of oppression on their continent that Jews experienced inside Europe. Both oppressions came from Christians and Christianity. Both peoples have special places in the European mind and in Christian theology as outside civilization and in need of conversion. To "civilize" and to "convert" means an affirmation of the life and religion of those with power.

Yet it is also a life and religion pervaded by doubt. The "other" inside and outside Europe and Christianity serve as a foil for the doubts of the powerful. If non-Europeans and Jews can be reduced to slavery and poverty, then this reinforces the sense that they are outside God's concern. Through conversion, the powerful are reinforced, for then the light—the light of Europe and Christianity—is found to be superior.

If our experience binds us together despite the "different" religions we hold, the religions themselves have to be interpreted carefully. The main distortion between the two revolves around Jesus. This places the question squarely before us. If our experiences in history joins us, can it be that the Jewish figure that Christians affirm as messiah also unites us? In response to the question I thought the following. Separation is a unity if the messianic interpretation of Jesus, militarized within an institutional structure tied to empire, is seen as a violence against indigenous peoples outside Europe and Jews within Europe.

The messianic Jesus was used to convert non-Europeans as part of the process of exploitation of goods, cultures, and indigenous religions. Within Europe the messianic Jesus was used to do violence to Jews, a deep violence that used the Jewish tradition against his own people. On the one hand, non-European and Jewish religion is seen

as in need of a messianic figure. This Jesus who was unknown or rejected by the suffering *was* known in absolute certainty by the powerful. Or was he? This absolute certainty is shadowed by doubt. Why
else the need to convert others to your way under pain of banishment
or death unless your own doubt is so strong?

I remember having some of these thoughts before I traveled to
Costa Rica, but the context of my lecture brought these thoughts to
a clarity that I had not expected. Richard translated my talk and af-
terwards we spoke at length about these insights. His own scholarship helped flesh out my own more intuitive sensibility.

As a biblical scholar involved in grassroots activism, he interprets
the Jewish and Christian traditions as two traditions. But these traditions are defined less by the question of Jesus and more by the realities of those who are powerful and those who are oppressed.
Accordingly, their continuity comes less from belief and more from
social and political context. Even the hope for deliverance is defined
differently by those in and out of power. Among the powerful deliverance from sin is defined abstractly. Among the poor deliverance
from oppression is needed concretely.

Richard defines the choice clearly. There are two Gods in these traditions. One is a God of death who is with the powerful. The other is
a God of life who is with the poor. The God of death transcends the
Jewish and Christian traditions, as those within other religions can
also embrace that God. The God of life transcends the divisions of traditions that emerge in history. In short, the God affirmed is the unity
rather than the different symbolic expressions that seem to divide.

For Richard, the Bible demonstrates this unity around the choice
between the God of life and the God of death. Involved in the world
around it, the Bible should be read in a "materialist" way. The Bible
is distorted when read as an anticipation of a messiah or a world beyond this world or as a reinforcement of Judaism or Christianity. In
the main the Bible records concrete struggles of local peoples for justice and compassion. God is raised up or argued against in relation to
these struggles. Much of the language of the Bible is earthy and direct. Much, too, is laden with symbolism, a coded vocabulary of the
struggle for justice.

This language is interpreted by those who come after within their
own systems of interpretation and in their context of material relations. Often the meaning of those who struggled is lost in religions

that emerge long after. *Judaism and Christianity come after the Bible.* They interpret and seek to structure struggles that have their own context and meaning. Therefore, the Bible is often distorted. The very notion of the Bible as old and new testaments and as the books of Judaism and Christianity belie this transposition.

Richard seeks to free the texts by looking at the history involved and the two traditions that claim and transform them into a false division. In biblical language, the division between the God of death and the God of life is much stricter than the division between Judaism and Christianity. The God who brings death is more accurately described as the God in whose name death is brought. This God is an idol. Richard defines idolatry as a false description of God or the use of belief in God to accomplish the subjugation of a people. Idolatry is the problem. Religions that foster idolatry do so to hide what is occurring in history. Religion becomes a way of producing and reproducing views of the world that allow or mystify oppression.

A typical response to religion as idolatry is atheism. Atheism is usually defined as a disbelief in God but, in Richard's understanding, atheism is the refusal of idolatry and the God in whose name idolatry is promulgated. Oppression of the poor is often justified in the name of religion, a religion sometimes held in common, either through inheritance or through affiliation. Thus the main struggle of the poor is with idolatrous religion. Their struggle is with false Gods rather than atheism.

Biblical allusions to this concrete struggle against idolatry are many. Richard cites prophets and books in the Hebrew scriptures, Jeremiah, Daniel, and the Maccabees, and in the New Testament, Acts, Corinthians, and Galatians. In these narratives Richard finds various arguments against forms of idolatry. In general, idolatry is named as that which is destructive of human beings, nature, and history. In particular, the idolatry of money, law, and oppressive political power is emphasized.

For Richard the central theme of the Bible is this struggle against idolatry. It is, at the same time, a struggle to separate the God of death and the God of life. The religious struggle is a political struggle to free God and the people from false belief and death. Where that struggle is, the God of life is present. Unity is found within diversity across time, culture, and geography; and divisions imposed by imperial religions are transcended by this unity. False unity im-

posed by imperial religion needs to be fought just as political oppression does.

So much of liberation theology is a prophetic call to return to the
sources of the tradition as a way of mobilizing the poor with the symbols forced upon them by the oppressors. Hence, the battle is over
the Jesus that both sides agree is salvific. One is found in a transcendent realm, the other is found here as a liberator. After the discussions with Richard, I realized that he poses a very different
understanding of the question. For Richard, Jesus' importance lies in
his identification with the God of life. In this identification, Jesus expressed the desire to free his people from the oppression of the Romans, that is, external occupation, and the Jewish religious
hierarchy, that is, internal occupation.

Judaism and Christianity as we know them formed after the
fourth century of the common era. For Richard they represent a reassertion of the internal and external control that Jesus, *in continuity with others before and after him,* challenged. The tragedy is that
the division that was developed over the millennia has been so suc-
cessfully reinforced by both Judaism and Christianity that even those
who accept the division Richard identifies often accept the separation of Judaism and Christianity as two religions.

Richard's proposal is radical. Jesus is not *the* messiah, rejected by
his people, against the Law and its strictures, inaugurating the kingdom of love. Christianity is not *the* religion of truth and salvation. It
is to be judged in the same way that Judaism, or any other religion,
for that matter, is judged. The witness against idolatry is the connection among Jews and Christians and those of any religion.

Richard is a provocative thinker. If Jews and Christians are linked
in their fight against idolatry, how do we articulate this connection?
Is this the collapse of all distinctions, a syncretism beyond the imagination? Does it mean, as I stand in front of the Central American activists and discuss with Richard, that we are together in a new
tradition that has yet to be named? How does one identify such a tradition? What rituals are there that bind us as a community? What
happens with the symbols and cultures that have grown up around
and with these religious divisions? Is the synagogue service to be replaced? Is the Mass to be said or forgotten? Is the return to the
"essence" of the tradition simply misplaced energy? Does it reassert
the division even in its search for an ecumenical age?

Richard asserts a continuity that is retrieved as it expands and moves into the future. The point is to cut across traditions and find the places of struggle and fidelity throughout history. In this process every tradition's claim to truth is challenged. To privilege any elements in one tradition over against other traditions is denied.

In the case of Christianity, the person of Jesus as messiah is relativized. So, too, the Jewish concept of chosenness. The traditions we inherit are de-centered. As a Jewish thinker without clerical responsibilities, it is easy for me to contemplate the ramifications of his analyses. The courage Richard displays as a Catholic priest is inspiring.

Perhaps the de-centering of any one tradition vis-à-vis others is inevitable when traveling and living the diaspora. Often in the de-centering process, however, elements within the tradition are re-centered. For instance, the claim that Jesus is the messiah is re-centered for Christians in an interreligious context. Likewise, some Jews today can affirm that the chosenness of Jews does not preclude the "chosenness" of others. De-centering can be a process of letting go *and* holding on at the same time. Sophisticated theological speculation emerges. This explains how Jesus can be a messiah for Christians and not for others. Or, more often, how the explicit recognition that Christians have of Jesus as the messiah exists among others without their knowledge. This is true for Jews when chosenness is seen as involving all peoples: the explicit chosenness of the Jews by God is followed by a chosenness as specialness for others. One involves God, the other, special cultural characteristics developed in particular histories. The ecumenical dialogue thrives on these understandings as a fallback position protecting the centrality of Judaism and Christianity in the modern world.

The de-centering Richard speaks of is different. It seeks a re-centering outside of any particular tradition and claim. It is not a joining of forces of these traditions to protect and expand their vision by emphasizing the need for continuity. Rather, it is seeing the traditions as containing a variety of elements that articulate this most important struggle *and* mask it as well. Religious traditions are famous for raising up in death those who unmask the tradition in life. In doing so they often co-opt movements that once threatened to destabilize the institutional structure of church and state.

De-centering the tradition and the elements within it avoids positing the projection of religiosity as an ontological event. It denies that any particular religion is somehow connected with God. Judgment of religion becomes similar to the judgment of society, employing political rather than theological criteria. Rather, the political judgment on religion and society has a theological component that unmasks religion and its institutions as highly political. The claim of a theological warrant is tested through the politics of the church or synagogue with regard to justice and peace.

The extension of Richard's analysis is clear. Any religiosity that is tested by this center will accompany the people in their struggle for justice. The interplay of religion and the people's struggle constantly de-center the claims of religion because they are active and engaged, challenged and challenging. By recognizing the elements of struggle across geographic, cultural, and religious lines, the solidarity of movements for justice de-center all claims of religious and political orthodoxy.

What, then, anchors the commitment for justice or gives solace and strength when political success is limited or when it fails? Though liberation theology emphasizes political engagement, the anchor remains God and the salvific work that Jesus began and his followers continue. An option for the poor and marginalized is claimed. But that option is grounded in the choice that God made to be with those struggling for justice, first with the Israelites and again through Jesus. Is Richard suggesting that people are willing to suffer and die for justice without the sense that God is on their side? Is liberation theology the religiosity that developed to combat the forces of oppression that claim God on their side?

As a theologian, Richard feels a responsibility to argue that God opposes oppression and accompanies those who struggle for justice. Because he is among people who affirm Christianity, his articulation of this God is within Christianity. When in a small town in the countryside outside San José, Costa Rica, he introduced me to a group of poor farmers and laborers who gathered for a meal and discussion at the local church, his words were carefully chosen: "My friend is a Jew from the United States who is traveling to learn more about Christianity and justice and thus more about Judaism and justice," he said. "We can learn more about the God of life and justice together."

In simple language a profound statement is made. Particularity is affirmed to understand where we have come from. Universality is explored to decide where we need to move toward.

کﺉ

AT THE CHURCH I asked Richard to inquire of the pastor, a priest from
Spain, if he knew where another Spanish priest, Joan Casañas, was
now located. Richard had published Casañas's essay in a book I read
some years earlier. I was profoundly moved by the essay and I rel-
ished the possibility of meeting the author. It happened that the pastor was a friend of Casañas for many years, but knew only that he had
returned to Spain. Richard knew Casañas briefly in Chile, as
Casañas was located there in the 1970s and left his parish setting to
travel with the guerrilla fighters opposing the Pinochet government.
Casañas's essay was a theological reflection on those fighters. Many
of them were atheists, at least as considered in the traditional sense
of the word.

What struck me as I read the essay was the incredible honesty of
Casañas's approach. He refuses to cover over the trials of the revolutionary fighters or to dismiss them. Instead he listens to their beliefs
and disbeliefs and confronts traditional Christianity and liberation
theology with their experience in the struggle for justice.

For Casañas the revolutionary fighters and the peasants who lost
loved ones in the various conflicts in South America have to be con-
sulted if any theology is to be taken seriously in the future. Revolutionary fighters give the ultimate commitment by setting their
minds, bodies, and hearts toward justice. Peasants are often caught
between the forces of the state, religion, and revolution. Like the
guerrillas they have no stake in the religious system as it is. Their
struggle and suffering challenge easy theological formulas from the
right or the left.

Casañas asks whether the bishops in Santiago, safely ensconced
in their villas with the protection of the state, know more about God
than the guerrilla and peasants in the countryside searching for answers to understand their own commitment and predicament. Does
the typical parish Catholic have a better understanding of God when
he affirms that God is in the Mass, than does the peasant who has
lost everything and cries out against that same God? The articulation
of liberation theology is also called into question when a mother who
lost her child to the military is broken in a way that no comfort can
relieve. For the theologian, Jesus is among the poor. For the person
in grief, God or Jesus may be absent.

If Jesus is among the poor, why the suffering without end? Casañas does not think that the more recent theories about the "crucified God, and the Father who refuses to act with force, and who suffers and sacrifices with the people until they are liberated from their oppressors" help to clarify the matter. Instead Casañas concludes that the question of God is elusive. He finds that many revolutionaries experience an "elucidation through abundance," an overwhelming sense of oneness and commitment. They do not have a formula for naming God. "It is difficult for us to live underway—always on the move—even when we have knowledge of the goal toward which we are heading, the name to be given it, and the manner of expressing it," Casañas writes. "But God is not; God will be. And if God does not exist yet, then ours is the task of making God exist (the task of intrahistorical justice), even without knowing what God is, or is like."

In my journey to Costa Rica different currents and perspectives mingled together. To the activists I said that we are joined in a tradition that transcends the divisive question of Jesus. To Richard I responded that I understood the broader tradition of faith and struggle he was articulating. Both helped clarify a sense that had been growing inside of me. The divisions handed down to us make little sense in the lives of the people who suffer loss. Nor can it mean much to those who seek to articulate a future beyond the cycle of destruction and death.

The church people who accepted me as a Jew from the United States demonstrated Richard's own understanding through hospitality rather than theology. They intuitively knew the way forward as one of hospitality, that is, the acceptance of one another in the context of the search for justice regardless of our different backgrounds or perhaps because of them.

Casañas challenged me as he invoked the possibility that the search for God is itself a search for justice. That the formulations of God are on the way to a realization that has yet to occur. There is no definition, only a glimpse, an attempt to name what cannot be named, especially when injustice is the norm. Can we live without certainty about God *and* with the knowledge that God is nearer or more distant on account of our actions and commitments? Is the abundance I feel a closeness to a God I cannot name? Is Casañas's "elucidation through abundance" the God I experience in traveling and living the diaspora? Is this the God I experience in exile?

The three strands of theology I experienced in Costa Rica—overt liberation theology, Richard's de-centering of the traditions through the question of the God of life, and Casañas's elucidation through abundance—captivate me. I search for a language to describe the interpenetration of these elements.

A search for language can become as theoretical as previous theologies, words about words and rituals to add more words. The activists, of course, were returning in a matter of days to their work where words are contextual and dangerous. Often as not, they are broken by violence and the words themselves ring hollow. Or, after some days together sharing theology and hospitality, they return with renewed strength only to experience this hollowness again.

I have met those who are broken by the violence. These are people whose commitment and faith have been tested and failed. New theology and the sharing of pain are no road back. This is the other side of martyrdom and perhaps one of the reasons for the raising up of martyrs. Destruction and death challenge humanity at a level where coping is sometimes impossible. Words and rituals fail.

Perhaps this happened to Casañas himself. The essay I read is the only essay he wrote, at least as far as Richard and I know. And the rumor that the Spanish priest confirmed is that Casañas has been broken by the deaths of the people he accompanied in the revolutionary movement he so beautifully evoked. Casañas traveled and lived the diaspora in a most remarkable way. He felt and articulated its contours without averting his eyes. He has affected my own journey in a substantial way.

I wanted to meet and thank him. I also wanted to hear his reflections on the exile he now traverses. It is an exile that he hints at, created a framework for, and now lives. I wonder if he experiences this "elucidation through abundance" in exile,

⋑

THE GATHERING in Costa Rica was energizing and haunting. The trajectory that Richard traced was liberating. It broke through a confinement that puzzled me. It also promised a broader sense of love's work. Richard brought together and articulated what was inside of me.

This was true with Casañas as well. When I read Casañas I experience a freedom that I long for. It is the freedom to be religious without mouthing a ritualistic formula or averting my eyes. There are no formulas or expectations, just life and its varied expressions. There is no tucking of words and actions into neat corners. I no longer feel the need to fit my life into predetermined patterns.

The continuity that Richard found, I acknowledge. The elucidation through abundance that Casañas writes of, I experience. The activist group I spoke to and the church gathering I attended in the countryside are experiences that remain within me.

And yet the diaspora I traveled is foreign. Its reality is not mine. Traveling and living the diaspora are essential for understanding at a deeper level where one is going. In the end, home is where the essential decisions are made and the fullness of life is lived.

Confrontation with the powers outside is important. It can also be a deception. There is an internal confrontation that can be enriched and postponed by traveling and living the diaspora. The Yom Kippur confession is important and insufficient at the same time. Practicing the externals without the internals is only halfway there.

The God of life is a broadening of perspective. Elucidation through abundance broadens perspective still further. Even this can be superficial, however, if the God of life and abundance becomes cliché, invoked to battle the limitations of previous discussions about God or used to battle the forces and personalities who oppose you. The cycle of violence and argumentation continues anchored in the same ground.

I found the attempt to escape these various cycles illusory. Humanity is grounded in the same earth. We have the same limitations and possibilities. Language varies in words and tones but structures remain. Though some languages express certain ideas and concepts in particularly enlightening ways, there is a boundedness in all language. So too with culture and religion. The use of all religions to envision a future is important and limiting at the same time. Because one day that broader understanding comes up against its own limitations and people search for a meaning more resonant with their experience.

Will the diaspora I travel and live be the diaspora those in the future experience? Most people living today have different experiences and the diaspora I see may not be the diaspora that others see. The exile within that diaspora is also my own.

Casañas's experience is haunting in this regard. A Spanish Catholic priest, he travels to Chile. In the midst of repression he understands those who oppose the dictatorship on their own terms. Or does he? What Casañas does is counter his own religious world, of which he is an official representative, with the world of the revolutionaries, who have also been formed within their world.

The world of the bishops and the dictator, the Spanish language and Chilean culture—liberation theology itself—is *their* world. Casañas investigates that world with insight and passion. He sees another place where this world can arrive. Casañas is a mediator of a world that is struggling to be born. He is broken in this birth.

Pinochet is gone as dictator and democracy is restored. The world of the revolutionaries, at least to some extent, remains unrealized. Injustice and division remain. They fought the fight necessary in their time. Some who survived the struggle are broken. Some remain committed to their dreams. Still others have changed, embracing what they once fought against. Is this not the fate of most revolutionary movements, to be defeated and thus scattered? To have won and thus be absorbed into the ways of the world?

The limitations of life and society are found in dictatorships, democracies, and revolutions. Those who ride the crest of the systems and movements flourish until another wave displaces them. Those thrown under, those who fight the wave that kills, are themselves often discarded or murdered.

I wonder what accounts for this brokenness. What can salve it? Does the exile always remain even when a common diaspora is recognized? Could it be that particularity becomes even more obvious when the diaspora is traveled and embraced?

The limitations *and* the depth of particularity come into focus during this journey. It demands a deeper reckoning. There is no way out of one's boundedness to time and birth or its manifold contradictions. Context, absurdity, strength, and limitation are all part of life's journey. Possibility is found within boundedness. Through exploration of that which is foreign and expansion of what is home, we become who we are. If through the journey, home is found to be relative and unequal to the task, it remains our home. It is constitutive of who we will become.

Thus the mistake of pretending we are the diaspora we travel or the exile we live. I am both. I am neither. We are participants in and outside of both. Is this also true of God? God can be found in the broader tradition of faith and struggle as Richard articulates it. This

God must be brought into existence as Casañas speculates so vividly. It is also true that God is needed in the particular and the now, in the smaller places and before justice. I have experienced this God in the brokenness and in silence.

Casañas warns that pious phrases should not cover over the absence of God in suffering and injustice. His own suffering heightens this alert. Still, the fidelity he describes and the fidelity that he lives may point beyond his own ability to embrace the present. Casañas's own brokenness points toward the here and now of God's presence. It is only by incorporating and moving beyond any one experience and articulation of God, or the inability to affirm God, that we come to grips with this most haunting and difficult question. But this also means transcending our own limited experience. The question of God can only be approached within and beyond what we know, experience, and learn. *God can only be experienced when the past, present, and future are freely embraced in our own lives and beyond.*

It is this lack of free embrace that has brought the Jewish search for God to a halt. It is this same lack that forces a return and a mysticism that lacks an honest reckoning with the present. This. is also the reason for the formulaic repetition of so much of contemporary Christian affirmation. Rebellion against the Constantinian aspects of both traditions is not enough for an affirmation that has depth and expanse. Mistaking paths chosen in the past for the possibility of God in the present happens often. This embrace of the past as a future makes it more difficult to find God at the end of Jewish and Christian history.

To have access to this broader tradition of faith and struggle, a difficult freedom is necessary. A difficult freedom has a sense of particularity and universality at the same time. While judging historical configurations of faith and power, it allows underlying themes and possibilities to speak within and across historical divides. Without this freedom, how can Jews listen to elements of Christianity, or Christians of Africa, Asia, and Latin America listen to those who come from Europe and North America? A discerning freedom sifts out history as it came to be and the possibilities that were defeated in that history. The cycle of injustice and atrocity is crucial here. So is the ability to envision a spirituality beyond that cycle. Freedom is retrospective only in its fight for a future; the future contains elements of the past in a configuration that has yet to appear. In this sense, along with Casañas, though with a caveat, God has yet to exist *for our time*. Our image of God is in the making.

Freedom to cross boundaries is itself a practice of discernment and forgiveness. Forgiveness is difficult because it signals a willingness to enter territory that has been hurtful in the past. Though difficult, there is no other way of traveling the diaspora. Exile itself is painful and the diaspora can be likewise a journey among strangers unless new relationships are built.

Can these relationships be glimpsed without the practice of mutual forgiveness? Forgiveness is a process of transcending the structures and beliefs that oppress and hinder a shared humanity. Forgiveness is oriented to the future. Standing in a similar place of freedom, on a path that promises a new commonality, forgiveness becomes revolutionary. It affirms brokenness *and* the possibility of a future that embraces and transcends that brokenness.

Perhaps God is found in brokenness and in the future, in forgiveness and in possibility. I wonder if these are the same places experienced at different times and sometimes together. Brokenness subverts present injustice as it also posits a future beyond brokenness. The future is superficial without the memory of brokenness. Forgiveness is ongoing if possibility is to have depth.

What is a future without humility, possibility without a sense of limitation, if not a repetition of the cycle that went before? The challenge for me is to open what has been closed, to free what has been chained, including the images I have of God. But if we are chained to the past and to the division found there, how is the image of God to be freed?

In the struggle with the God of life and the demands of forgiveness, the covenant remains. *Only now the particularity that has surrounded the covenant is shorn.* The texts, languages, institutional memory, and ritual that surround the covenant only point toward or away from the embrace we seek. Different religions contain testimony to the ongoing search for the covenant. They point toward a terrain of embrace. They are not the embrace itself.

The broader tradition of faith and struggle expands the possibility of embrace and places it in a new configuration. Those who have testified in the past by speaking and living their encounter with humanity and God are seen within a broader spectrum. Their particular discipline can be culled rather than held up as *the* way to be replicated.

Testimony is what we have. It is our way of encountering life in its hope and possibility. Where does this testimony lead? Is this testimony, as Walter Brueggemann suggests, the core of biblical Israel in the land and outside of it, within the promise and in exile? Is speech that affirms God's presence or laments God's absence the same affirmation that God is and will be as promised in ancient times and now? Brueggemann argues that the testimony, countertestimony, and complaint of biblical Israel is what we know of God. Affirmation is the fulfillment of Israel's sense of God as Israel's complaint is in anticipation of the return of God's promise. This is less a systematic exposition of a theology of God than it is a traveling testimony of an Israel who is sure of God's presence in that journey. This certainty continues even when lament is the order of the day.

Though notably chastened, the core testimony remains. Brueggemann suggests that it is in the exile that the core testimony about God is most deeply affirmed. There is little reason to speak about God in trial and tribulation if the disappointment itself is not a reminder of God's presence.

I wonder if this is true of prayer as well. In his study of the prophet Isaiah, Daniel Berrigan suggests a somewhat different sense. "The effect of the prayer of the morning is simply that life goes on," Berrigan writes. "Perseverance is the only answer. There is nothing spectacular, no breakthrough. But for all that, prayer will not be silenced, even by the silence of God." Berrigan ponders the millennia of prayer that links our prayer to the time of Isaiah and before. "The beat goes on. We have great ancestry, holy rabbis, teachers. Shall we have descendants to match them?"

Berrigan suggests that testimony is our daily presence in peace before God, in argumentation with God, and, at times, without God. Testimony means that I am present and open. Still, questions remain. Am I summoned to be present? Or am I present because I am human? The testimony of morning prayer is our presence because, at least for Berrigan, it is constitutive of the human.

Yet Berrigan also affirms an essential element of Brueggemann's understanding when it comes to faith. "One has not really (that is, in the biblical sense) said in one's heart, 'God exists' until one has said, 'I trust you,'" Berrigan writes. "The first assertion is notional, abstract, a matter perhaps of natural theology, the mind laboring at its logic. The second is communion, bread on the tongue from an unseen hand. The first can be uttered in all good faith, even as one takes the contrary evidence as decisive. . . . The second is a heavy burden of denial of all that: 'You have spoken, I cannot know the outcome. I obey nonetheless.'" Berrigan affirms a foundation for the ritual of morning prayer in the sense of trust that is without knowledge or verification. Is this trust also constitutive of the human?

In exile, traveling the diaspora, the questions of testimony and prayer take on these elements of presence and trust. But this can only make sense within the context of being called and sent: "You have called, I obey nonetheless, we will not be silent even if You are. Life goes on." The sending is now expanded beyond Israel's testimony as is the content of morning prayer. The broader tradition of faith and struggle contributes images and words that elucidate, change, and sometimes contradict that testimony. It is almost as if the biblical sensibility is behind us *and* before us, always alert and open to new coloration and dynamic.

Isaiah remains a witness in the biblical canon. More importantly, he becomes a witness in the discipline embodied in the movement forward. "I obey nonetheless." This is my response to a God who is sometimes present and other times absent. "I continue on without fear of crossing the boundaries of religious divisions, without fear of losing the 'foundations' of my inheritance and upbringing." This is my response to a humanity that is sometimes just and other times engaged in injustice. For me, obeying nonetheless must be in response to *and* in spite of God *and* humanity.

Where does this testimony lead me? It has led me to the places that a Jew is not supposed to go, to Christians, Germans, Palestinians, and beyond. But I am also aware that these labels define religions and peoples in categories that are ultimately abstractions. Labels are part of a journey, places of entry where the other is encountered. If there is an other, how else are we to encounter it than through the larger lens? Testimony is amplified. The encounter is articulated in terms that are noticeable and dramatic. Controversy and applause are in the air. Something has happened out of the ordinary.

Testimony is more difficult to discern when the other is no longer other. Categories are broken through. The diversity of the other reminds me of the diversity of the sending community. When the other becomes intimate in friendship and culpability, then the challenge becomes more difficult. Testimony then is less public and the issues between and among peoples begin to dissolve. Is there such a thing as the Jewish people or the Palestinian people? Do the categories Jew, Christian, and Muslim really suffice to explain the deeper aspects of the person?

Individuals exist. We are formed by history and are free to evolve within the present. Traveling the diaspora relativizes and enhances the communal aspects of life. They appear as important and as illusions, formative and distant. Testimony is received and created. It is dispersed into the larger world as a practice that informs the person and yet is so limited as to defy definition and importance. Is this the same for prayer and for God? That my struggle to be faithful is known only within? Is it important to speak of this in the larger world except as a curiosity to those few who take notice?

Testimony emerges from a practice that grounds us in the world. It deepens our own struggle to be faithful. It is a life given to the world through an interior sensibility that has no wish to be recorded and no hope of becoming part of a new scripture. The practice itself becomes the foundation from which a life is lived without a sense of success or the knowledge of changing the world. Can it be that my testimony has no known destiny or direction? It could be that my testimony has no known destiny or direction—that it is neither denied or affirmed by God.

Prayer is ultimately an act that allows the letting go of destination and destiny. So it is with the testimony we inherit and create. It is a reality and a creation but its end is also unknown. It hovers, it can be touched, it is palpable. It is also elusive, like air surrounding us, untouchable.

Testimony becomes part of the future as humankind continues to struggle with the questions that confront each generation. That which seems disparate and aimless is one day gathered together by those who come after. This is what the canon is, the gathering and interpreting of a previous struggle to be faithful as if it is defining for all time. The mistake of the canon is the freezing of the testimony. Our testimony is no less valid than the testimony that precedes us.

I wonder if my own experiences will be gathered together or lost to history. Will they remain hidden and known only to the few? Perhaps they will be interpreted within the old canon, contributing to renewal even as I argue against it.

Epilogue

IN 1995, MARYKNOLL CLOSED THE DOORS of its school of theology. I had taught there and developed a program in justice and peace studies there for fifteen years. But more. I lived a life of travel and encounter. Where else can I teach a Tanzanian during the morning and have lunch with a visitor from China? At Maryknoll cross-cultural interaction is intense and sustained. The people who came to Maryknoll were committed to justice in their own countries. These commitments carried a cost. After their studies, I was often able to visit them and learn at a deeper level of their concerns and contexts. At Maryknoll, I was a teacher. Even more I was a student. Issues were focused and alive. The word in the classroom was also a word to be brought to the world.

It was not all beautiful by any means. Maryknoll is alive with commitment and disputation. The role of the missionary and the entire concept of evangelization are issues of great moment. They are hardly academic. Maryknollers commit their lives to mission work. It is a vocation rather than an academic discipline. When the question of mission is discussed everything is at stake.

But Maryknoll was also dying. Or rather it was dying and peculiarly alive at the same time. The 1980s especially carried this paradox to its extreme. The seminary had already begun to decline. The seminarians were fewer and fewer. Their quality was questionable. The community was becoming older and soon more than half the Maryknollers would be beyond retirement age. Since Maryknoll is self-sufficient and a family, increasing attention had to be paid to its elderly. Over the years of my tenure there, Maryknoll increasingly took on the aura of an extended care facility.

Yet signs of life abounded. A lay missionary program was in full swing and Orbis Books, a publisher of liberation theology from the Third World, was in full stride. The commitment of Maryknoll was known all over the world and when the sisters were murdered in El Salvador the community name and witness became a national story. When I traveled to give lectures on various topics I, like other people associated with Maryknoll, was followed by reporters.

The same fall that the sisters were murdered, Dorothy Day passed away. She was eighty years old and the Mass was held in the local Church of the Nativity, where Dorothy had been a daily communicant. The church was in the same neighborhood as the Worker and the poor and wealthy, the known and unknown, gathered to honor her with a memorial Mass. I was invited and came down to the city to pay my respects.

It was a diverse group that gathered there. Cardinal Cook had wanted the Mass to be in the cathedral where he would officiate but Dorothy had wanted a more simple church setting. She made a statement without stating it directly. She identified with the church of the poor rather the established church of the wealthy. A compromise was reached. Cardinal Cook greeted people as they arrived at the door of the church. He left as the Mass began.

The great Jewish radical Abbie Hoffman was there, as was my teacher William Miller. It was typical of him. He drove in from Milwaukee and was in the overflow crowd outside. I arrived with Gene Toland and was escorted inside the church. When I saw Miller outside the church I asked him to come in with us. He declined and waved me on. I reluctantly entered the church without him.

Miller was a humble man to be sure and a traveler of the diaspora until his death. Raised a Southern Protestant Christian, Miller became one of the first historians of the South after World War II. The question of faith haunted him, and his contact with the civil rights struggle and a local Catholic Worker in Tennessee carried him to the threshold of the Catholic Church.

How different he was from my other formative teacher, Richard Rubenstein. Rubenstein is bold in his thought and assertive. He carries himself as an important thinker, one to be dealt with seriously.

In some ways he is a forbidding man and the stories about Ruben-stein's responses to trespassing on his turf are legendary. Miller was just the opposite. A shy man, Miller rarely spoke in public. In an intellectual battle he withdrew. He became the center of attention by refusing the center.

By the time I studied with him, he was through with the academic side of teaching. Though he continued to teach classes, he refused academic convention. His lectures were short on facts and often had nothing to do with the topic at hand. He repeated himself endlessly. The bourgeois world is doomed and the thought that comes from such a world is abstract and deceptive. The challenge is commitment and the timelessness of the community one joins in that commit-ment. He quoted the Russian philosopher Nikolay Berdyayev and re-cited verses from Henry Adams. The great beast is time itself and only outside of time can community be embraced.

My graduate work with Miller was short on class work and heavy on reading and writing. His mode of teaching was hospitality. On the long winter nights in Milwaukee, Miller would call me and ask what I was doing. That was his invitation to the long car rides we often took together. He would arrive at my apartment and we would drive for an hour or so to some unknown destination. Then, just as we had arrived, we would turn back and return home. During our drive we would speak about subjects of importance. We would also be silent. When I would ask him his opinions on faith, suffering, and the Holo-caust, he demurred. He listened to me as I searched. He accompa-nied me in silence and hospitality.

When I think back to those days at the Catholic Worker, Mar-quette, and Maryknoll, I think of my youth and those who challenged and were patient with me. They seemed to understand part of me that I would come to know much later. And yet I wonder if Ruben-stein or Miller would ever be hired to teach in a university now. Their eclectic thoughts and eccentric behavior might not be acceptable to the academic orthodoxy of today since probing questions of commit-ment rather than arcane trivia is not as highly regarded.

Meeting Dorothy Day and living in the same community with her for a year, beginning to know Daniel Berrigan in my university years and then at Maryknoll as a lecturer in my program, rubbing shoulders with James Cone and Gustavo Gutiérrez at Maryknoll over the decade of the 1980s—all of this was an experience that unfolded without intent.

And then there is Rosemary Radford Ruether, the great Catholic feminist theologian, who accepted my invitation to teach one summer at Maryknoll. From that moment, and even more in the 1990s, we traveled together around the world especially for issues relating to Israel/Palestine and the Jewish-Christian dialogue. I have never met a more selfless person, especially one who is known and can use her name to justify distance and assertion, which is not to say that Rosemary is meek. In engagements during the first Palestinian uprising, persons in the listening audience would often violate canons of civil engagement. Though I agreed with her point of view and was often attacked myself in the same way, sometimes I felt like protecting the questioner from her quick and decisive response. Like Dorothy Day, Ruether is a great mind and a caring person. To see either as an absorbing listening post, however, would be a mistake. Humility and openness should never be mistaken for a meekness about commitment and truth.

The years after Maryknoll were difficult, and the clarity of exile—indeed the origins of my memoir—came within one of the most prestigious institutions of higher learning, Harvard University. For the better part of three years I held appointments in the Center for the Study of World Religions and the Center for Middle Eastern Studies. I met the well-placed and the intellectually arrogant but I also met the humble and the exiled. I remember particularly Hilda Silverman and Sara Roy on the Jewish side and Elaine Hagopian and Saud Dajani on the Arab side. Hilda is an unsung hero, always working on the fringes of the Jewish community and building bridges with Palestinians. For the most part her work is unrecorded and volunteered. Sara is likewise on the fringes, though her name is publicly known. A child of survivors of Auschwitz, she travels among Palestinians and analyzes the economy of Gaza. Like Hilda she crosses boundaries in solidarity. But Sara has a further internal boundary to cross. Reaching out to Palestinians is a question of justice and healing in a public and personal way. Could her outreach be one of personal healing for the crime against her parents?

I met many Palestinians and Arabs at Harvard who are in a double exile today. The first is from Jewish power, the other is from the corruption of the Palestinian Authority and Arab governments that survive by oppressing their own people. How different the other looks when met in their humanity! I witnessed in these Arabs and Palestinians a future awaiting birth.

Would this future be stillborn? Did the glimpse of this future decrease my sense of exile?

At Harvard my sense of exile increased because the reality of life was closing in on me. I could come to Harvard, but in the world of academic employment, difficulty abounded. As a committed Jewish thinker, one would think the academic world open. Once restricted from employment, Jews are now welcome and sought after. Some of the most prestigious and well-paid positions in the humanities are in Holocaust and Jewish Studies. These positions are almost exclusively reserved for Jews. Jews are also found throughout the upper levels of academic life, including in the administration of universities. In my travels seeking employment, I found that the number of Jewish deans, provosts, and presidents is great. It is not just the Ivy League schools that have this presence. Universities in the Midwest and the South also have this presence. Of course, Jewish money in these universities is ever-present and the search for money from any source is a priority that few universities can afford to ignore or alienate. This is also part of my learning in my travels in the diaspora: Jews have made it in society and the academy.

It is good that this is so, but like our empowerment in Israel and America, it carries a cost. The cost is thought itself or at least the radical thought that poses unthinkable questions that, often as not, set the next stage of a people's journey. One of the most difficult aspects of my journey has been witnessing the decline of the Jewish intellectual tradition. Our empowerment has occurred in my lifetime; so too has the diminution of Jewish thought. At one time we had to fight Christian domination to think and act publicly as citizens. We struggled against Christianity to place our historic and religious journey in the public realm as legitimate and self-sufficient. My own struggle has been against the forces in my own community in the space that has been ceded to Jews and redefined by Jews.

⌐t

OVER THE YEARS of my travel to Israel/Palestine I came into contact with many Palestinians, including a small and formidable Christian community gathered at St. George's Cathedral located in the heart of Jerusalem. The community's pastor was Naim Ateek, an Anglican priest. Like Elias Chacour who responded to my talk in Jerusalem, Ateek is both a Palestinian and an Israeli citizen. His family was displaced from his native village, Beisan, in 1948, but, partly because of its Christian background, his family was displaced to Nazareth. Nazareth became part of Israel, hence Ateek's dual identification as Palestinian and Israeli.

I initially met Ateek at my Jerusalem talk. Like Chacour, he had been asked to respond to me. Ateek refused because he had heard many liberal Jews speak and he had grown tired of hearing a rhetoric of peace that had little to do with justice. After some persuasion he consented to hear me. I noticed his presence immediately. In a crowd of over two hundred Jews, he was one of a handful of Palestinians in attendance and his clerical clothes also caused him to stand out. The points I made in my talk surprised him, especially my call for confession and reparations to Palestinians. Afterward, he sought me out and invited me to his home the next evening.

I was one of the first Jews in his home and the hospitality shown me made what could have been a tense encounter a pleasant meeting. At the end of the evening he brought out a manuscript on a Palestinian theology of liberation. He asked me if I would read it and tell him what I thought about its quality. That night I read the manuscript straight through, excited by the possible connections of a Palestinian and a Jewish theology of liberation working in tandem. The next morning we spoke and I asked if I could take the manuscript back to Maryknoll to see if Orbis would publish it as a book.

This was the beginning of a friendship that has now spanned more than a decade. It has been a working friendship and more. Orbis agreed to publish the book and asked Naim, now a friend, to come to Maryknoll for several months and do some editorial work in preparation for its publication. Since that time we have traveled throughout the Middle East together and to different parts of the world. We have lectured together too many times to count. We have also spent a tremendous amount of time together on a more personal, even pastoral level.

It has not always been easy for either of us. Though Naim's English is perfect and we speak together freely, he is from a different culture and religion. As someone who has experienced Jews almost exclusively as oppressors and liberal Jews in particular as patronizing and sometimes duplicitous, Naim's ability to trust Jews is relatively weak. At the same time, his Christian theology evolved in a context that forced a conservatism foreign to my sensibility. At the beginning at least, Naim's Christian theology was supersessionist and in his writings his estimation of Judaism as alive, viable, and informing, was low. In fact, more than a few theologians in America chided me for speaking to and with him, especially in public forums. Jews did not like it because Naim's Palestinian voice is too strong. Christians in the ecumenical dialogue did not like it because his supersessionism reminds them of the theological tradition that they now repudiate as anti-Semitic. They see the path of this history as leading to the Holocaust.

Could my solidarity with Palestinians be tempered because of a Christian theology that I, too, repudiate? The undertones of mistrust could also warn me away. Present in a Western Christian I would immediately challenge that person. Was this my role here? Or could this be overcome through an ongoing relationship of solidarity and risk?

Christians in Israel/Palestine are caught between two aggressive religions backed by theological and political power. The first is Judaism, militarized in Israel and supported by religious leadership in America. The other is traditional Christianity. The Western Christian fantasy of Jewish aggression culminated in the Nazi theories of a global Jewish conspiracy and the biological spoiling of Aryan blood. Christian understandings of Jews were also mind games of deicide and corruption. But Palestinian Christians experience Jews in reality as aggressors and murderers. When they speak of "the Jews" in a tone of disgust, they point to those who spell destruction of home and homeland. As a Jew traveling the diaspora, it was initially difficult for me to adjust to this mythical, hateful, and blood-stained language that I read about in history or even heard, sometimes in coded language, in the West. Though it grated on my ears, the reality for Palestinians is clear. Jews are exactly this for them and when I listen to mothers whose sons have been murdered by Israeli soldiers, it is not within me to start a sophisticated theological discussion. I am humbled by the pain I hear and my own complicity. They tell me a truth about my people's return that no argument can dismiss.

Thus my commitment and our evolving relationship. Over time Naim started a Palestinian theology center in Jerusalem named Sabeel. In Arabic, *sabeel* means the way or spring of water. I had visited Sabeel on numerous occasions since its inception in 1992. In 1998, Sabeel hosted an international conference on the subject of Jubilee. The timing was thought through carefully. Israel was celebrating its fiftieth year of statehood. Sabeel posed the question of the meaning of the Jubilee year, an event that is featured in the Hebrew Bible.

Jubilee is a time of rest and celebration. It is found in the weekly calendar on Shabbat, as a marker of the seven days of creation. Every seventh year a sabbatical is declared and in the fiftieth year as well. In the seventh and fiftieth year, rest is balanced with justice and celebration with a leveling of society. The biblical theme is a reflection on the societal inequalities that have emerged in the previous years with the understanding that the quest for justice is more than a social and political ideal. It is fundamental to a people who claim a divine mission. The revisioning of society is also the revisioning of God. In Judaism this is the God who led the people from bondage into freedom.

On the fiftieth anniversary of the founding of Israel, a celebration of the Jewish community was expected. But the Palestinians demanded the justice that is integral to the event. Would there be religious content to the celebration, a radical redistribution of land and power? If that did not occur could people really celebrate the Jubilee?

I was asked to speak to the issue from a Jewish perspective. What does the Jubilee mean at this point in Jewish history? What would I propose for it to mean? What actions have to be taken to make the Jubilee real and efficacious?

The conference was held in Bethlehem, mostly because Jerusalem was essentially closed to Palestinians who lived outside the city. Part of the Oslo myth was that with peace the borders are open. In fact the sealing of the borders that became official a few years later was already in place. The center of Palestinian life was closed. If Palestinians were to attend, the venue would have to be outside Jerusalem.

I was invited to be one of two speakers on a panel discussing the history and contextual application of the Jubilee in Israel/Palestine. The first speaker was Rabbi Jacob Milgrom, an extremely prominent biblical scholar. I would follow. A discussion would ensue.

Rabbi Milgrom outlined the origins and elements of the biblical Jubilee in a detailed way. He included the relevant analysis: geographic, economic, political, and societal redistribution so that justice can become the rule of the land rather than injustice. God is the author of the Jubilee and the worship of God is dependent on this cycle of reflection and leveling of inequality. Milgrom also included the stranger in this analysis, though he was somewhat vague on the relation of Jews and others in the land itself.

Milgrom is older. He came to Israel a few years earlier to spend his retirement years in Jerusalem. His son had been in Israel for many years and now he wanted to fulfill what he considered to be his obligation to the continual evolution of a Jewish state. Milgrom is obviously an American and his son remains deeply so as well. After many years of traveling to Israel/Palestine I am used to seeing the American Jews who have settled in Jerusalem and other parts of the land. In fact, Rabbi Milgrom lives in a Jerusalem that has been unified and annexed unilaterally—and illegally, according to international law—in the wake of the 1967 war. He, of course, does not understand his neighborhood to be a settlement, but the Palestinians who attended the conference certainly do. He could easily travel from Jerusalem to Bethlehem and back. Many of the Palestinians were stuck inside or outside of Jerusalem. They were becoming strangers because of policies of dispossession and settlement, not because they were originally so. Could Milgrom make the case that he recently arrived from California and is indigenous to the land, whereas those Palestinians confined to Jerusalem are strangers?

In questions after his talk, Rabbi Milgrom found it difficult to respond to this strange inversion of native and indigenous that questioners raised. It was not spite or even anger. It certainly was not for want of intelligence, education, or compassion. In his early seventies, Milgrom was clearly a good man with the best of intentions. Milgrom was simply unable to conceptualize the Palestinian point of view. All his rabbinic and biblical training did not prepare him for the simplest and most concrete of conceptions. His new environment, literally built on top of Palestinian land and culture, did not advise him a problem existed.

I began my presentation with a turn of categories. I simply suggested that the Jubilee be applied to all who lived in the extended community of the nation. Justice for all, land for all, redistribution of economic and political power for all in the land. A shared land and society is already a reality, except in an unjust arrangement. Isn't the Jubilee a time for the righting of the wrong and the new beginning that the holy year is supposed to represent?

My own perspective was simply to extend to others what we ourselves want: ordinary life, some semblance of equality and justice, the ability to participate in public life, respect for culture and religion. Milgrom did not disagree, nor would he want to, in any case. His entire being is oriented toward this view and in any place except Israel he would argue for this extension to all. Hadn't he been raised, educated, and been respected in an America where the extension of welcome to Jews had made some Jews refer to it as the promised land?

Milgrom could not deny this logical extension; he could not affirm it either. He was without malice or category. He became confused. As a Jew I quickly realized his difficulty, and as a person I felt for his situation. In many ways he is a tourist for his remaining years, living in Jerusalem but not really living there. Or living in a planned community that, like the planned communities that have become the rage in the United States, are comfortable and artificial. They are planned to keep reality at bay. Indigenous culture is fenced off; geography is transposed. The planned community is there and not there.

In the audience was Naela Ayed, a Palestinian health worker whom I had met many years ago at Marquette. I was working on my doctorate in history and she on a master's degree in public health. She was the first Palestinian I ever met and during her last months there we often met and talked. During the years of her further graduate work at Johns Hopkins, we would periodically meet. Naela was full of life. She had an ironic sense of humor and an openness to culture and difference. A secular Muslim, she nonetheless respected religiosity. Despite her experiences with Jews in Palestine she was always open to me. Our friendship evolved far beyond politics.

She was a born and bred Jerusalemite. The city was her home and after I lost touch with her I would periodically inquire about her when I traveled to the Middle East. Each time I inquired it was either too late to visit or she was abroad at a conference. But this time we met. It seemed then and even more so now like fate.

When I arrived at the hotel in Bethlehem, there was a message from Naela waiting for me. She had seen an advertisement for the conference some weeks earlier and noticed my name on the program. She asked me to call her so we could meet during my visit. I reached her by phone and soon she arrived at the hotel. The next days were spent attending the conference and catching up on news and happenings in our lives.

Naela had returned to Jerusalem a few years previously, determined to work among her own people. Her field was health and development and she worked primarily in the West Bank as a consultant to the Palestinian Authority and international agencies. Her experience with the Authority was less than encouraging. She was disappointed with the Authority for a variety of reasons. There was a lack of professionalism in the administration and corruption was also in evidence. She experienced a general lethargy within the ranks as the needs on the ground grew more desperate. I had heard the same feelings from other Palestinians. An initial excitement about the possibility of peace had turned into a widespread feeling of betrayal. Some felt the Authority to be a new occupation, selling out the interests of the Palestinian people for private gain and power.

Naela also came back to fight for Jerusalem. When I visited her home in Jerusalem I found it located in a beautiful and strategic location. Right outside the Old City of Jerusalem, you could see the Dome of the Rock from the road outside her home. Just down the road from her home was the small textile factory that her father owned and now her older sister ran as a family business. I visited her sister there and she pointed to the vacant lot next to the factory. She and her family also owned this land. Both pieces of land were valuable beyond their market worth. As it turns out, a settler group backed by wealthy Jewish financiers desired this land. They wanted to start a settlement there so as to lay further claim to the entirety of Jerusalem. Naela and her family refused to sell on principle. Jerusalem was also Palestinian. This land was part of their claim. It was their birthright.

Naela was always pleasant. She was a determined person who, like many young Palestinians, had to create a life within the context of dispersion and exile. She had traveled the diaspora and was open to new experiences and the various cultures and values she found there. In the process of traveling, she also strengthened her particularity. Thus she combined an openness and a commitment.

We spent an entire day talking together at her mother's home. Her mother is quite a character. Though she appears a traditional Palestinian grandmother, some of her views are decidedly nontraditional. I was particularly taken with her love for the rock star Madonna. When Madonna gave a concert in Tel Aviv, a friend secured Mrs. Ayed tickets. Her description of the concert and her love for Madonna remain with me and each time I hear Madonna's name or see her image I think of Naela's mother.

After some time together, our discussion turned toward the political situation. I noticed then a toughness in Naela that I had not experienced before. She was agitated; she described Palestinians and Jerusalemites as being pushed into a corner. So much had been lost over the years of occupation and more was being lost during the peace process. The writing was on the wall and Naela was ready to fight. Like many Palestinian professionals and activists, Naela was a determined secularist and, of course, a woman who prized her independence and freedom. Perhaps this is why she had never married. Yet if she had to don traditional Islamic women's garb as a protest against the loss of Jerusalem she would. Her response to Milgrom after his talk also followed the same line. She upbraided him for his ignorance and presumption. She only barely contained her anger. Everything was at stake.

The last time I saw her was at the concluding dinner for the conference. I invited her and her sister. She enjoyed herself and so did I. The following day I flew home to America.

When I returned the following year, I asked my hosts if they would call Naela's mother and arrange for me to visit. Naela was often out of the home and her mother spoke only Arabic. My lecture was in the evening. My host told me she would call in the morning.

The next morning I inquired if the call had been made. My host's face was somber. There was something that needed to be said, but how to say it? I was curious. Was there a problem? The answer was stunning. Several months after my last visit Naela was murdered. I was stunned and had to sit down. Murder was something I read about in newspapers. In all my travels in the Middle

East, all my acquaintances and friends had remained alive despite the various uprisings and wars. Some of the people I met had been jailed. Some had been tortured. Others had barely escaped harm. Murder is irrevocable.

I immediately asked if I could visit with the family at her home. I didn't know whether they would remember me and if, as a Jew, I would be welcome to pay my condolences. They accepted to receive me and soon Naela's older sister came by with her car.

The drive through Jerusalem was difficult. Naela's sister was distraught and I hesitated to speak. What could I say to the sister of a friend who had been murdered? My presence brought back Naela's memory. My Jewishness could not help but open other wounds still fresh and deep.

Mostly, we drove in silence. The arrival at Naela's home was even more difficult. What would I say to her mother, a woman so deeply in grief that no words or gestures could assuage it? So I sat there in silence until the tears were shed and the discussion of the murder filled the room. Pictures of the funeral service were brought out; people in the pictures were identified and the Palestinian and Islamic symbolism was explained. Accusations were also made: the murder was clearly political, relating to the property that Naela's family owned and Jewish settlers desperately wanted.

I was the first Jew to come to Naela's home and pay condolences to her family. And afterward, I was the first Jew to visit her grave site.

Naela's grave is right outside the walls of the Old City, near Zion gate, where Muslims believe the first of the dead will rise on judgment day. Because of the age of the cemetery and its desirous location, coffins are buried one on top of the other and family plots are opened to make room for the newly deceased. But Naela's coffin is sealed, never to be opened until judgment day, because in her death she was declared a martyr. Her martyrdom was a witness unto death of steadfastness, of resistance, of dignity in the face of oppression. As I placed my hands on her tombstone, I wondered if in her life Naela had been carrying the covenant with her. I contemplated this thought in silence, a silence that the tears of her sister deepened and pierced. As I left, I silently prayed the Sh'ma and thought of the Kaddish, the Jewish prayer for the dead, both prayers intoned by so many Jewish martyrs in history and over so many Jewish grave sites.

In the hotel later that night, I thought of the experiences I have had and the many that I will have in the coming years. Most of them are hidden to the world, perhaps meaningless in the larger scheme of things. Even in the circles of religious thought and justice, most of these experiences are lost in frameworks of understanding that belittle those who are outside, in the "wrong" places, or even on the side of a history that is, at least for now, unrecognized. What categories allow us to remember together those Jews and Muslims in exile—Etty Hillesum, Gillian Rose, and Naela Ayed? Is the secular Palestinian Muslim buried outside the walls of Jerusalem to be remembered along with the Maryknoll sisters murdered in El Salvador? What am I to do with the memory of the Holocaust that makes invisible the memory of Naela, as if she were just a footnote, an unfortunate victim in a larger drama of innocence and redemption?

The new diaspora is full of people like Naela and Etty and Gillian and the sisters from Maryknoll. We remember the grave sites of our own and of others. Are these other grave sites also our own?

In the morning, Jerusalem is beautiful and thoughts of the tragedy of history—missed opportunities for justice and reconciliation, senseless death that leaves a void and misery, traditions that are squandered in crime and complicity—drift into the soft sky. In the morning, even the militarism of righteousness, so present in Jerusalem over the millennia, has not yet fully awakened. That is how I experienced the morning after my visit to Naela's home and grave site. It was a great sense of gratitude for her life and for the witness of a possibility beyond the cycle of violence and atrocity, a way grounded in the ordinary respect for life and peoples that Naela and so many others have died in witness to.

Where is God in this tragedy and gratitude? Is one dependent on the other? Is God involved in both? Sh'ma is Hebrew for listen, or hear. Do we listen to or hear God's word? Does God listen to or hear our word? Do the cries of the martyrs move God to compassion? Do the cries of the martyrs move us? The Kaddish speaks of the coming kingdom. Do we see that coming kingdom in the exile, in the evolving new diaspora, in the hidden histories that surround us? In the practice of exile, after traveling the diaspora, we are left with the ancient prayers and hopes that seemed so inadequate, that are chanted so hypocritically and are so often the cause of pain and suffering.

I remain here with many others in between the known and the un-known, the ancient and the new, practicing exile in the new diaspora. In exile I have constructed a home that is always on the move; a pilgrim and a witness to death and to the possibility of life. Once chosen, exile is like a fate that is embraced and celebrated, against the odds of history and sometimes even in the face of common sense. We cannot be faithful for the sixteenth century or the twenty-third century; only in our time do we have the possibility and the opportunity. And we cannot prove the accuracy or the efficacy of that fidelity. We can only live that fidelity to the fullest, reminded of our own flaws and limitations, and without any expectation of earthly or heavenly reward.

Books Quoted

Berrigan, Daniel. *Isaiah: Spirit of Courage, Gift of Tears.* Minneapolis: Fortress Press, 1996.

Brueggemann, Walter. *Cadences of Home: Preaching among Exiles.* Louisville: Westminster John Knox Press, 1997.

Casañas, Joan. "The Task of Making God Exist." In *The Idols of Death and the God of Life: A Theology,* edited by Pablo Richard et al. Translated by Barbara E. Campbell and Bonnie Shepard. Maryknoll, N.Y.: Orbis Books, 1983.

Frankl, Victor Emile. *Man's Search for Meaning: An Introduction to Logotherapy.* Part one translated by Ilse Lasch. New York: Washington Square Press, 1984.

Rose, Gillian. *Love's Work: A Reckoning with Life.* New York: Schocken Books, 1995.